Centre for Educational Research and Innovation (CERI)

Ministry of Education, Ontario
Information Centre, 13th Floor,
Mowat Block, Queen's Park,
Toronto, Ont.   M7A 1L2

THE EDUCATION OF THE HANDICAPPED ADOLESCENT

THE TRANSITION FROM SCHOOL TO WORKING LIFE

ORGANISATION FOR ECONOMIC CO-OPERATION AND DEVELOPMENT

Pursuant to article 1 of the Convention signed in Paris on 14th December, 1960, and which came into force on 30th September, 1961, the Organisation for Economic Co-operation and Development (OECD) shall promote policies designed:

- to achieve the highest sustainable economic growth and employment and a rising standard of living in Member countries, while maintaining financial stability, and thus to contribute to the development of the world economy;
- to contribute to sound economic expansion in Member as well as non-member countries in the process of economic development; and
- to contribute to the expansion of world trade on a multilateral, non-discriminatory basis in accordance with international obligations.

The Signatories of the Convention on the OECD are Austria, Belgium, Canada, Denmark, France, the Federal Republic of Germany, Greece, Iceland, Ireland, Italy, Luxembourg, the Netherlands, Norway, Portugal, Spain, Sweden, Switzerland, Turkey, the United Kingdom and the United States. The following countries acceded subsequently to this Convention (the dates are those on which the instruments of accession were deposited): Japan (28th April, 1964), Finland (28th January, 1969), Australia (7th June, 1971) and New Zealand (29th May, 1973).

The Socialist Federal Republic of Yugoslavia takes part in certain work of the OECD (agreement of 28th October, 1961).

The Centre for Educational Research and Innovation was created in June 1968 by the Council of the Organisation for Economic Co-operation and Development for an initial period of three years, with the help of grants from the Ford Foundation and the Royal Dutch Shell Group of Companies. In May 1971, the Council decided that the Centre should continue its work for a period of five years as from 1st January, 1972. In July 1976, and in July 1981, it extended this mandate for further five year periods, 1977-1981 and 1982-86.

The main objectives of the Centre are as follows:

- *to promote and support the development of research activities in education and undertake such research activities where appropriate;*
- *to promote and support pilot experiments with a view to introducing and testing innovations in the educational system;*
- *to promote the development of co-operation between Member countries in the field of educational research and innovation.*

The Centre functions within the Organisation for Economic Co-operation and Development in accordance with the decisions of the Council of the Organisation, under the authority of the Secretary-General. It is supervised by a Governing Board composed of one national expert in its field of competence from each of the countries participating in its programme of work.

Publié en français sous le titre :

L'ÉDUCATION DES ADOLESCENTS HANDICAPÉS
Le passage de l'école à la vie active

© OECD, 1983
Application for permission to reproduce or translate
all or part of this publication should be made to:
Director of Information, OECD
2, rue André-Pascal, 75775 PARIS CEDEX 16, France.

This study would not have been possible without the generous assistance, in the form of a grant, from the United States Department of Education, Office of Special Education and Rehabilitative Services.

Also available

THE EDUCATION OF THE HANDICAPPED ADOLESCENT: Integration in the school (August 1981)
(96 81 02 1) ISBN 92-64-12229-X   150 pages   £3.80   US$8.50   F38

Prices charged at the OECD Publications Office.

THE OECD CATALOGUE OF PUBLICATIONS and supplements will be sent free of charge on request addressed either to OECD Publications Office, 2, rue André-Pascal, 75775 PARIS CEDEX 16, or to the OECD Sales Agent in your country.

In recent years significant developments have taken place not only in the education of young people with disabilities in school but also in their preparation for and transition to adult and working life. There have been substantial shifts in attitudes and policies but there is a relative lack of evidence of current practices and research. In 1978 the Governing Board of the Centre for Educational Research and Innovation (CERI) of the OECD took the view that attention to the adolescent stage was particularly called for as more work had been done in relation to provision for younger children considered handicapped and because concern about employment prospects for the disabled was universal. A project entitled "The Education of the Handicapped Adolescent" was therefore initiated that year with the aid of a generous grant from the United States Office of Special Education and Rehabilitative Services.

In the last four years many Member countries have contributed by documentation and participation in seminars to a consideration of the two themes given priority in the project, namely integration in the final years of schooling, and effective strategies in the transition of young people with handicaps to adult and working life. A report on the first theme has already been published under the title <u>The Education of the Handicapped Adolescent - Integration in the School</u>. The present publication on the second theme of transition attempts to summarise trends and innovations and illustrate them with specific examples.

This book is aimed not only at those responsible for developing, administering and providing services at national and local level, including those working in schools, colleges, sheltered workshops and social welfare services and those in voluntary organisations, but also the handicapped themselves and their families.

Two people have made major contributions to this study, both in terms of writing major sections and overall editing: they are Mr. Barry Taylor, Chief Education Officer, Somerset, and Consultant to the CERI, and Mr. John Fish, formerly Senior Inspector, Department of Education and Science, United Kingdom and now part-time consultant to the CERI on the programme on the Handicapped Adolescent.

It should be noted here that this report covers a wide and complex area which will need further enquiry. This will be carried out by the CERI in a programme on transition to working life of young people with handicaps, again supported by a very substantial grant from the United States Department of Education.

CONTENTS

Introduction 9

Part One

AN OVERVIEW

I. The Objectives of Transition................. 16
II. Enhancing Employability...................... 22

Part Two

REVIEWS OF SOME TRANSITION PROGRAMMES

I. The Years of Schooling and Transition to Work in the Département de l'Orne, France.
G. Grey, Education Officer, Somerset Local Education Department, England............... 46
II. Work Training in the Département de la Somme, France.
M. Davies, Senior Education Officer, Buckinghamshire, England......................... 61
III. The Integration of Pupils with Serious Learning Difficulties into Normal Working Life in Norway.
K.M. Helle, Work Research Institute, Norway 75
IV. The Integration of Handicapped Youth in Italy.
Dr. V. Bagnasco, Servizio Minori, Provincia di Parma 88
V. Developing Vocational Opportunities for Handicapped Persons.
Dr. G. Thomas Bellamy, University of Oregon 98
VI. Employing the Handicapped in Swedish Industry.
A.M. Quarfort, Göte Bernhardsen, Swedish Government Commission on Long-Term Employment..................................... 112

VII. The Roles and Needs of Parents of Handicapped Adolescents.
Peter Mittler, Sally Cheseldine and Helen McConachie, Hester Adrian Research Centre, University of Manchester............ 127
VIII. Alternatives to Work for the Handicapped.
Professor Jack Tizard, Dr. Elizabeth Andersen, Thomas Coram Research Institute, London....................................... 152

AN OVERVIEW OF THE PROJECT NOW COMPLETED.......... 187

INTRODUCTION

The CERI project "The Handicapped Adolescent" sets out to study many of the complex issues which beset the individual with a disability during the final years of schooling and the transition to adult and working life. As well as international discussion of common concerns, examples of successful practices in different countries were identified and used as a basis for the exchange of information and ideas in meetings and seminars. Finally the knowledge was further extended by the dissemination of the results of new approaches and practices.

The method has been to commission studies in most, if not all, of the participating countries and use these as basic documentation for seminars, arranged by national authorities with the Centre, on aspects of particular significance to them. Countries holding seminars included Australia, France, Japan, New Zealand, Sweden, Switzerland, the United Kingdom and the United States and all included widespread international representation. One of the last acts of dissemination goes even further: it has been to procure the production of three half-hour television films - in France, Italy, Norway - concerned with the integration of handicapped students into ordinary schools and the problems of their entry into working life.

The work of the project has concentrated on two major themes:

i) the integration of young people with handicaps into ordinary schools during the last years of schooling, and
ii) their transition from school to adult life.

Results of work in the first of these themes has already been published by the OECD in "The Education of the Handicapped Adolescent - Integration in the School". The second provides the substance of this volume.

The method here has also been two-pronged. First, as a result of contributions to various professional seminars and discussions within them, it has been possible to assemble an overview, defining common problems and examining approaches to them in Member countries. This is presented in Part One where eight topics are examined, namely:

- curricula in the final years of schooling;
- work preparation and vocational orientation courses beyond school;
- careers advice and personal counselling; relationships between the education system and
- potential employers;
- sheltered work;
- modification to the working environment;
- the enhancement of employment opportunities;
- facing unemployment.

The bulk of the book, Part Two, continues the work of dissemination by giving a wider readership to a selected number of reports and case studies. These have been drawn, inevitably, from a minority of the countries and the individuals who have contributed to the analysis and interchange of experience that has taken place over the past four years.

But first, it is necessary to make a few observations about the scope of the work, the limits to the overview and the definitions being used.

Coverage of the Project

We can be reasonably sure that in most countries the percentage of the population with disabilities, or significant difficulties which might be handicapping, is greater than those for whom special provision is made in childhood and adolescence. For example, in the United Kingdom between 1.5 per cent and 2.5 per cent of children are placed in special schools or units and another small percentage receive some special help in mainstream schools. On the other hand, research has demonstrated that between 10 and 15 per cent have learning difficulties arising from a variety of causes which require special help for at least part of their school career. In the United States 9 per cent of the school population is assumed to require special education, but the numbers receiving such help vary from State to State.

A precise definition of the extent of disabilities and significant difficulties in the population is seldom possible since criteria vary and the availability of services may influence statistics. Thus in this report definition has been consciously avoided but the presumption is made that the project is concerned with 10-15 per cent of the population and not simply those who, at the end of the school period, are receiving special education as defined in the country concerned. However, the incidence of handicapping conditions does vary between different communities even in the same region.

While it has been appreciated from the outset that social and economic disadvantages are inevitably associated with sensory, physical and mental disabilities, and are particularly crucial during the period of transition, no attempt has been made to include handicaps arising solely from those disadvantages. This issue was discussed by participants some of whom were anxious to include socially and economically handicapping conditions. Within the international context it was, nevertheless, decided that work should be concentrated on those young people with physical, mental or emotional handicaps. In part this was to avoid duplicating the work already being undertaken by other international organisations concentrating on social disadvantage, but also there was a general feeling that activities could become too diffuse and consequently of less value to practitioners in the field.

Definition of Terms

In recent years there has been a marked move away from specific labelling or categorization of handicaps, partly because no one system is appropriate for all the professions concerned or even the whole age range, and partly because improved assessment has indicated a larger percentage of those concerned as having a combination of disabilities and difficulties. This trend has been recognised within this volume with a clear presumption that a descriptive approach to an individual's special needs together with a prescription of the services, experiences and methods required to meet them, drafted jointly by education, health, social welfare and other professionals together with parents, is the right way forward.

The age span covered by adolescence and by the period of transition is not easy to define chronologically. For the former a wide span between the final years of compulsory schooling, say 12 or 13 years of age and 19 or 20, has been assumed. However, the period of transition presents greater difficulties since the age of leaving the school system and entering employment with or without an intervening vocational preparation period varies markedly in Member countries. In some countries a relatively small percentage of the target population remains in full-time education beyond the compulsory period, while in others the majority may do so. For example, in Sweden those who are mentally handicapped are likely to remain in school until 21 years of age and in other countries young people are still in the transition stage at this age.

The transition stage can, however, be seen to have three phases, at whatever age they occur:

i) the final years of schooling and the steps taken to prepare for leaving school,
   ii) transitional arrangements including vocational preparation and the first period of working life, and
   iii) to the maximum extent possible, independent living.

It is with all these stages that discussion and examples in this volume are concerned.

The Desire for Work

A common problem revealed by the project is the percentage of this layer group who are considered in any country to be severely and profoundly handicapped. Criteria are uncertain, means of providing a significant life with meaningful occupation are less well developed, but there is a constant thrust from their families and advocates for education and training opportunities which develop their capabilities to the full and normalize their lifestyle.

In most participating countries the point is made with increasing force by self-advocacy movements and voluntary organisations. The rights of the disabled are increasingly asserted both by them and by others, often relatives or friends who group together to speak for them. The case made is not wholly, or usually even primarily, a financial one; more fundamental is the quest for self-esteem, an acceptable place in society, personal fulfilment and integration within the community - and for all of these, a regular job is seen to be the threshold of personal achievement.

There is, of course, another compelling motive for the disabled to seek work. Even in those countries with the most highly developed social welfare system, the unemployed are likely to be amongst the poorest members of society. Equally the relationship between disability and relative poverty has been well catalogued. For example, in 1978 in the United Kingdom 32 per cent of adult handicapped males were officially judged to be below the poverty line, a far higher proportion than for the general population, and 62 per cent of single disabled women bore this additional handicap.

Low incomes not only affect the material standard of living but often the quality of life to a greater extent because of the implications of particular disabilities. Dependence upon parents, other relatives, support organisations or institutions is likely to be increased; mobility can simply be too expensive to achieve and social life virtually ruled out.

Nor are generous disability pensions more than a partial answer. Such payments often, quite unfairly, carry a stigma and rest on identifying underprivileged groups, amongst the physically or mentally handicapped, for "special" treatment. Thus pensions have, customarily, an adverse impact on self-esteem. In Sweden during the early seventies there was a dramatic improvement in the scope of the disability pension scheme. Yet in spite of this the disabled in Sweden are as determined, perhaps more determined, than those of other Member countries in demanding the right to work.

Obstacles to Work for All

Throughout the project a number of barriers to employment have been identified. Some of these relate to general conditions within societies and others to the nature of disabilities. At the same time a number of key issues have crystallised which influence the effect of these barriers. These include the curriculum in the final years of schooling, special work preparation schemes, counselling and social welfare supporting arrangements and modifications to the working environment.

The first and sometimes perhaps impenetrable barrier is, obviously, the severity and variety of disability of the individual. At one extreme are those, usually the severely and multiply handicapped, for whom even sheltered paid work is not commonly achievable, at the other those mildly disabled who with appropriate training can play a full role in an unmodified work place; the vast majority, which it must be remembered will probably be between 8 per cent and 15 per cent of school-leavers, fall somewhere between.

However, it is clear that in all countries the overwhelming majority of the group defined as handicapped are perceived as capable of holding down a job - if one is available. It is this factor that has given a new urgency to the issues of work preparation and the level of training and sheltered workshops which should be provided. Increasingly the general scarcity of jobs is putting pressure on sheltered workshops to accept young people who formerly would have gone into open employment but if not taken into a workshop have no alternative to idleness. Obviously every youngster of this kind who is given sheltered employment displaces someone more severely disabled, unless there is slack in the system, which is virtually unheard of. Yet to increase the number of sheltered work places appears to negate the universal desire to maximise the integration of the adult disabled into normal society. The problem is further exacerbated in most countries by the increasing proportion of the most severely disabled who in the last few years survive into adulthood as a result of medical and other advances.

The broader issue of the extent to which all handicapped people should be supported by social and other agencies within the community is universal. Exceptional treatment, whether in the educational system or via enhanced social welfare provisions - financial or otherwise - can so often insulate the disabled individual against the normal pressures and challenges of society, thereby sapping, not enhancing, independent living. Clearly this consideration is central to an almost universal desire, often as opposed to realisation, of the handicapped and those who are their advocates, for integration within mainstream school systems. But the unemployed will usually be an unrelieved financial burden upon the state's resources - unless they undertake voluntary work, which is still relatively rare amongst the disabled. Costs will be at their highest where institutionalisation is deemed to be necessary; the US Association for Retarded Citizens has estimated that this can be as high as $400,000 during an individual's life-span. But the combined total of unemployment benefit, other social welfare payments and support services for those living in their own homes, whilst less dramatic, are by no means insubstantial.

Part One

AN OVERVIEW

I. THE OBJECTIVES OF TRANSITION

Moving from childhood, through adolescence, to adult life is a transition all experience with varying degrees of help from families, schools and colleges, local communities, social services and employers. It is a mark of developed countries that this transition has become extended and more difficult. Education and training take place over a longer period, life choices are varied and the competences expected of adults to live and work effectively are increasing in complexity. Such societies have been increasing their expectations of citizens who in their turn are seeking greater participation in decision making and more say in matters which affect their lives.

The major components in a successful transition may be summarised as appropriate education, opportunities for acquiring an acceptable degree of personal autonomy, preparation for a social lifestyle including personal and recreational pursuits and an ability to earn one's own living. There are barriers on the way to maturity and full citizenship which can handicap the individual, many of which are economic and social in origin. Others, as in the case of those who are the subject of this study, have disabilities which make it much harder to achieve full participation in society for a variety of reasons. The principal one is that a reasonable degree of personal autonomy and economic independence is, for them, much harder to achieve. It is for this reason that arrangements during the transition phase are so important and central to these arrangements is preparation for a useful working life.

Why Work?

"I have been unemployed for 20 months and am very depressed; no one seems to want me, I'd be better off dead". So spoke a disabled youngster to his careers counsellor last year in a part of the United Kingdom suffering less acutely from unemployment amongst school-leavers than most others. In doing so he captured the basic reason why participants in the project have assumed that education and training must, above all, maximise the disabled young persons' ability to get a job. Even more than those without disabilities they look to work to provide a sense of purpose and usefulness as well as the social contacts which may only be possible through working. Another handicapped adolescent said: "I'm 18 and haven't got a boyfriend - I might if I went to work". It is the totality of dependence upon work to provide life's satisfactions which so often distinguishes those with handicaps from their contemporaries.

While paid employment remains the principal criterion for mature adult citizenship and status in society, it is not surprising that it is of such wide-ranging significance to those who are disabled. "Work makes you feel you are normal like everyone else and gives you self respect".

In most developed countries unemployment has increased and young adults have been most affected by more limited job opportunities. The idea that individuals can achieve reasonable status in society even if unemployed has yet to gain widespread acceptance. It requires great self-assurance for most young people to accept unemployment and considerable inventiveness to lead fulfilling lives without the disciplines and opportunities of work. Those with handicaps have difficulties enough in achieving an acceptable place in society and certainly they, and the voluntary organisations who speak for them, are in no doubt that useful work should be the object of transition. To add the objective of significant living without work to the other burdens of disability is seen as wrong and manifestly unfair. For this reason preparation for employment remains an essential and central feature of the transition from school to adult and working life.

Separate provision, whether before or after the statutory school leaving age, is being increasingly questioned and only supported when it clearly creates graduated experience for those with disabilities to develop experiences, skills and independence outside the relatively sheltered communities of special schools, colleges or workshops.

In the same way social welfare agencies and hospitals have in recent years deliberately undertaken programmes to develop the skills of independent living. Yet the risk remains, that unless these programmes are started at an early age, the more universal the caring service, the greater the possibility that some of those who are handicapped and their families will be reluctant to venture into the unfamiliar environment of work and independent living.

It is this factor rather than the financial and other safety nets provided for the unemployed by all Member countries in varying degrees, which can militate against a positive determination to seek employment. As has already been remarked there has been no indication of a reluctance to work on the part of the disabled because of lack of financial need - just the reverse.

Structural Unemployment

The availability of employment is declining for everyone at a time when more disabled young people are recognising the importance of work as the key to their participation in society and when new technologies are increasingly used to rehabilitate severely handicapped people. In the past three years only Austria and Switzerland have not suffered a substantial increase in unemployment among school leavers.

Agriculture, which has traditionally provided employment for many of the least academic school leavers and for many who are mentally retarded, has contracted its labour force. For example, in parts of the United Kingdom the labour force has shrunk to half its size of ten years ago even though production has increased. Equally important, mechanisation and more sophisticated management have demanded higher qualifications and skills from reduced labour force. The number of routine and unskilled jobs in industry, commerce and public services has declined markedly. The impact of microelectronic technology is only just beginning to be felt but its implications for employment have already been experienced in Japanese car making and Swedish shipbuilding. This structural change is almost certainly irreversible and all the governments of developed countries assume it will continue, often with increased momentum in the next few years.

The influence of these trends on the employment prospects of all young people has yet barely been recognised and for the wide range of disabilities and difficulties encompassed in the group of young people considered handicapped the effects may result in more barriers to a useful working life.

Recession and the Emergence of the Third World

The period which the project has spanned has coincided with the deepest world-wide recession since the Second World War. The hope is that this, like earlier recessions, will pass, that it is part of the conventiona cyclical pattern. In any case Western Europe, North America and Australasia have, in general, seen every successive recession of the past 10-15 years accompanied by progressively worse unemployment levels and a less satisfactory improvement as the recession has receded.

The disabled form a disproportionately large proportion of the unemployed and therefore recession bears particularly hard upon them. In 1977 a survey conducted in the United Kingdom by the National Children's Bureau identified 19.1 per cent of handicapped school leavers as unemployed compared with 4.4 per cent for school leavers as a whole. Three years later general unemployment had more than doubled and it is probable that a deterioration in the prospects for the handicapped had occurred in ratio.

This is not the place to attempt far-reaching speculation about the future of the economies of the developed countries or their relationship with the Third World. However, it must be extremely unlikely that the generally buoyant economies of 1950-70, dependent as they were in part upon a plentiful supply of cheap raw materials from the under-developed countries, will easily be re-established. Consequently the extremely high employment enjoyed by many countries during those 20 years may have gone for good. The disabled are not now virtually the only people to face long-term unemployment in many communities but have to compete for amelioration of their difficulties, for special programmes and for positively discriminatory employment policies with large and increasing numbers of contemporaries.

The High Cost of Labour

In recent years the cost of labour has become an increasingly dominant factor in the economies of individual firms, in providing public services and in the calculations of national governments. Thus productivity is all, not only in manufacturing industry but equally in the offices, schools and hospitals of central and local government, where substantial reductions in expenditure can only be achieved by shedding staff. The more labour intensive the operation the more crucial is optimum productivity. Yet many of the disabled, whilst perfectly capable of meeting the demands of a particular job, will take somewhat longer to do so. The blind shorthand typist, the mildly mentally handicapped retail sales assistant or the physically disabled data processor, may be simply unable to meet the work rate norms demanded by management and which often provide the basis for piece rates or bonus payments for a whole group of workers. No doubt many disabled would be prepared to acknowledge this and accept a slightly lower rate of pay rather than not have a job; but this raises extremely sensitive issues about the "rate for the job" and "cheap labour" discrimination and so on. It is not a practice which commends itself, understandably, either to trade unions or to disabled advocacy groups.

Yet the ever greater emphasis placed upon maximising productivity often militates against the employment of even the mildly disabled. One consequence is an even more profound dilemma as to whether individuals with particular disabilities should be pointed towards, and trained for, only those occupations where their productivity can match the non-handicapped. To do so would be a negation of the recent progress in many countries in opening up a much wider range of career opportunities and could encourage a retreat to the "ghetto" approach, back to, for instance, piano-tuning or basket-weaving for the blind.

Lack of Educational and Training Opportunities

In March 1978 the Australian Schools Commission called for "effective all-round training so that all handicapped people can acquire the skills needed to become contributing self-sufficient members of society". The Commissioners recognised that vocational training begins "as soon as children begin to talk and to count" and that the attempt to distinguish between general education and vocational training is quite artificial. Therefore, the quality of teaching and learning throughout the educational process, both at school and post-school, will be fundamental in determining a youngster's employability.

Yet the opportunities available to many of the handicapped, particularly after the statutory school-leaving age, are often grossly inadequate. In 1977 the Warnock Committee set up by the United Kingdom Government to investigate educational provision for children with special needs, learnt that whilst 29.2 per cent of all young people remained in full-time education after the legal leaving age, only 5.6 per cent of those handicapped did so. Some institutions of higher education have made notable efforts to accommodate those who are handicapped, particularly the physically disabled, but in general the picture is a depressing one. The able young handicapped person who graduates, qualifies as a lawyer or a doctor is much remarked upon but even amongst the highest levels of intellectual ability there are proportionately far fewer of the disabled realising their full academic potential.

The general position amongst those of average or somewhat above-average ability is likely to be as, if not more, inequitable, whilst those of below-average ability are unlikely to have any access to education or training beyond the statutory school-leaving age. Admittedly in some countries the pattern is altering; now all education authorities in the United States must categorise the further educational and training opportunities on offer to the individual handicapped school leaver. But generally, whether provision is integrated or separate during school years, afterwards too often nothing is done to enhance the handicapped individual's employability - and this at a time when the non-handicapped are receiving, and heeding, the clear message that post-school qualifications are more and more important in the battle for jobs.

There is increasing evidence too, notably in the United Kingdom, that the provision of special work experience and preparation courses for the young unemployed is less universally achieved for the disabled than for others in spite of examples of good and successful practice in this respect referred to later in this review.

In the context of a generally bleak outlook for post-school opportunities, there is the further dimension as to whether the objective ought to be to provide places for the handicapped on normal further education and training courses, or to construct specially designed programmes to meet their particular needs. Clearly any rational policy must be a fusion of the two but the special provision often seems easier to get off the ground in post-school institutions, although there are then the twin attendant dangers of narrowing the focus of job possibilities and not allowing full rein for the potential of the more able handicapped students. Increasing pressure on further education and training places in many countries from more qualified school leavers than can be accommodated militates against the development of special arrangements to enable those who are handicapped to take their place on the normal spread of courses alongside their non-handicapped contemporaries.

Attitudes of Employers and the Workforce

Throughout this project, the sympathy of individual employers has been highlighted as a crucial - and often the most crucial - factor in the job placement of the disabled. Whether or not a country operates a quota system or a disabled persons register appears to have relatively little impact on employer attitudes. Of more importance are contacts with former teachers, careers counsellors and the initial impression created by the handicapped themselves.

F.A. Koestler, commenting upon the situation in New York to the Public Affairs Committee, said, "the average person has no hesitation in contributing to philanthropic causes that benefit handicapped people but thinks in entirely different terms when asked to accept a disabled person as an employee or fellow worker. Pity instead of equity, charity instead of opportunity, indulgence instead of accountability - these are attitudes that are stumbling blocks on the road to equal opportunity". In other words a substantial educational task remains in modifying attitudes of the non-handicapped towards the less fortunate members of society. In this respect the thrusts towards the integration of the handicapped at school level in many countries might be expected to produce changes, although inevitably the process is likely to be a lengthy one.

In the meantime co-ordinated efforts of all those whose task it is to help and support the handicapped through the period of transition from school to work will be the key determinant in encouraging employers to give the disabled a chance to prove themselves, in proposing modifications to the work environment and accepted working conditions and in ensuring that the potential workmates are ready to accept the disabled and help accommodate their disabilities.

II. ENHANCING EMPLOYABILITY

The main objective of this book is not simply to define the difficulties in normalizing the future life and enhancing the employment prospects of school leavers who are handicapped. Although the considerations outlined in the previous chapter provide an important background to the evolution of realistic strategies, it is the positive aspect of the project which should be stressed. As the examples which follow this chapter illustrate, the project has identified examples of good practice from which much can be learned. Seminars and papers written for it have illuminated issues of wide significance and illustrated principles of general relevance.

There are, however, no universal panaceas, because the variables are almost infinite. The legislative framework of the particular country, its divisions of national, regional and local responsibilities between different services, social attitudes, the general availability of work and ways in which handicaps are defined in nature and severity are only some of the more obvious. Nevertheless, in recent years there has been an almost universal acceptance that society has a responsibility to accord full citizenship to those who are handicapped and within this context to maximise work opportunities. In the United States, for example, this has been earmarked in Sections 503 and 504 of the 1973 Rehabilitation Act which extend to people who are handicapped the employment- and service-related civil rights enacted earlier for ethnic minorities and women. The vocational and residential segregation of those who are handicapped are thus challenged as were "separate but equal" educational arrangements for black children. Other countries have extended the "right to work" principle to those who are disabled, even those who are severely handicapped, notably in Scandinavia.

For a number of reasons it is not possible to identify a common approach adopted by all countries. Among these are different patterns of responsibility for the post-school period involving education, health and social services, significant differences in the percentage of young people remaining in full-time education after the compulsory period and a wide variation in entitlements to benefits, pensions and training and supportive programmes. Nevertheless, most countries now try to provide opportunities after school ranging from day centres with a welfare emphasis, through various forms of sheltered workshops and supporting arrangements in the ordinary work place, to open employment. Often it is assumed that those who are handicapped will "flow through" these environments as their competence is enhanced by training and practice from the most restricted to the least restricted environment. However, there are several reasons why this does not occur in practice. Individuals stick at various stages because their independence or their productivity develop to only a limited extent and there is a tendency to retain effective operatives in sheltered workshops to maintain production; but above all the effect of more limited employment opportunities makes the outcome of successful training procedures much less certain in terms of paid employment.

If this approach, involving an assumption that the primary aim of all transitional arrangements is useful work and maximum autonomy, is to succeed, there must be a determined and co-ordinated effort to enhance the competence of all who are disabled from the earliest years. The rest of this chapter will consider this process under three sections - the school period, transition and the early years of working life - although it is recognised that each stage is dependent on the others and that a continuity in approach is important to success.

The School Period

Before turning to some of the common and essential ingredients of education in the final years of schooling, two major issues merit consideration, educability and integration. Very few of even those with the most severe handicaps are now excluded from what is recognisably an educational setting. For at least ten years there has been a general acceptance, at least among educators, that all are educable. In 1971 responsibility for children with severe degrees of mental retardation passed from the health to the education services in England and Wales. Local education authorities became responsible for the education of all children in these areas. Similarly, in the United States, Public Law 94-142 made free public education available, for the first time, to all children, however severely handicapped. These developments have not been paralleled elsewhere but even where responsibility remains with health and social welfare authorities the importance of an educational programme is now recognised. Thus in considering transitional arrangements we assume that there is no cut-off point at the lower end of the range of competence, however handicap is defined.

The general thrust towards integration has been recorded in the OECD publication "The Handicapped Adolescent - Integration in School". In many countries more young people who are handicapped are being educated in association with their contemporaries in ordinary schools, although separate special schools continue to play an important part in some of them. Integrative arrangements are seen to offer social advantages and, certainly for the more able, improved access to a wider range of academic courses. It is also argued that experience in the ordinary school may reduce the gulf that a young person with a handicap may have to cross between school and employment because he has become familiar with many more of the demands of everyday life than exist in special schools.

It is not at all clear that integration of itself facilitates employability. Indeed in some countries the programmes evolved in special schools have been very successful in preparing young people for transition to the world of work. In widespread and dispersed integrative arrangements it is by no means certain that the needs of individuals and small groups can be met effectively and their potential fully identified, let alone analysed. The design of curricula for small groups with specific disabilities may not be easily achievable. Nevertheless, it is widely appreciated that the special school environment can be more protected and cut off from the mainstream unless special measures are taken. Thus the imperatives of the transitional process urge strongly for the maximum normalisation of the school setting, along with the realisation that course design and work preparation tailored particularly for those who are handicapped may be much more difficult to achieve within regular schools.

There appears to be a consensus as to the key elements of the curriculum in the last three years or so of compulsory schooling. Predictably these are, as for other young people, the enhancement of communication skills, including numeracy, social education programmes, out-reach into the wider world and the maximum connection between home and school. Aesthetic and physical aspects are given more variable emphasis from country to country and school to school.

The crucial factor is, of course, the way in which these general features are translated into activities within and outside school. Perhaps most important of all is the preparation given to assist the handicapped youngster leave the sheltered and protective environment of school - and perhaps family - and cope with the threatening and unpredictable environment outside. Programmes in the last two years at school will often have not only this objective but also the parallel one of assessing what is the best destination for each pupil.

Major components, in addition to continued attention to literacy and speech are likely to include health, hygiene and safety, mobility and competence in the environment, personal development including personal relationships, self care, familiarisation with community facilities, social welfare services and the range of employment opportunities and alternatives to employment.

The extent to which the curriculum should be vocationally oriented, both in general and the particular, is the subject of considerable debate. The debate also relates to the extent to which such concerns should be included within the last years of compulsory schooling or in programmes which follow particularly where a high proportion of the school population enter such programmes. Most young people may be introduced to the routines of work e.g. familiarization with the disciplines and restrictions of work places, time-keeping, travel and how to apply for job. There is more marked variation in the emphasis given to specific preparation for particular kinds of work. In some countries this is uncommon; in others, such as the example from France which follows, there is preparation for fields of work, and in yet others specific skill training occurs in the last school years. On balance, general preparation tends to be favoured including familiarisation with fields of work since it is argued that too early concentration on a particular job may restrict the school leaver's range of opportunities.

In general, then, curricula before leaving school are not job specific. There is usually a throughgoing attempt to develop skills, knowledge and attitudes which will stand the youngster in good stead whether he subsequently lives at home or not, and whether he is employed or unemployed.

For administrative convenience most countries group young people with handicaps in categories or develop criteria for entry to different courses. Most of what is said in this book is general to all, but there are some issues where the nature and degree of disabilities are relevant to the school programme. For the purpose of this discussion three kinds of problem are dealt with separately. They are: young people with mild and moderate degrees of mental retardation, those with severe and multiple handicaps and those with sensory and physical disabilities. It is not suggested that these are discrete categories and they have many educational needs in common. Nevertheless, a focus on each of these groups in the last years of school illustrates different aspects of preparation for transition.

<u>Mild and Moderate Mental Retardation</u>

The first group is the largest single identifiable group in schools, whether special schools or not, although obviously many have additional disabilities, not least social and economic ones. The characteristic obstacles to learning are, by middle adolescence, limited communication skills, poor concentration, lack of confidence, and, often, a culturally impoverished background. A typical two-year programme designed to ameliorate these problems might include the following key elements, and many models of this kind which take no account of artificial subject divisions and may be covered by two or three teachers and sometimes one, have been identified in a number of countries.

Getting on with People

This element, or something very like it, is seen as fundamental, not only by teachers but also careers counsellors and potential employers. As well as the importance of listening, conversing, telephoning, writing letters and so on, understanding the other person's point of view is stressed. The disciplines of all societies, including the work places, are prepared for by examining routines and rules in school. The making and keeping of friends and the sharing of possessions and interests is also explored as well as the more mechanical social skills of entertaining and running a party. Much of the methodology is based upon observation of people working together in school and the work place as well as playing together. This element is also seen as the base for the development of moral concepts and notions of law, order and justice.

Citizenship: This element covers the institutions and practices of the young person's local community and the knowledge and skills required to understand and participate in them. Local studies and practical experience are essential. Young people may attend local committees and groups, visit a wide range of community facilities and organise activities such as charity collections, clubs and outings.

The Family: This is often a difficult area when throughout the developed world up to one third of the school population may live in single parent families or come from broken homes. Nevertheless, personal and social development within a family context, parental skills and similar topics form an important part of preparation for an adult role in society. At the same time the links between families and welfare services are explored.

Home Management: This area envisages that personal autonomy for both boys and girls will include the ability to care for themselves in their own home in adulthood. Cooking, care of clothes, planning and budgeting are common topics as are the ramifications of setting up home.

Social Arithmetic: A study of financial and related issues for young school leavers by the Lothian (Scotland) Education Department runs to seven closely typed pages illustrating the complex pattern of employment and welfare payments. In many developed countries wage, tax and benefit systems are complicated and courses need to cover these topics in addition to shopping and money management, including banking and saving and knowledge of the common domestic and transport measures and timetables.

Employment

All curricula, in varying ways, deal with choosing a job - security, conditions, pay, hours, companionship and working life. Usually an attempt is made to relate educational and personal qualities to various jobs and here there is a bridge to the careers counselling normally provided from outside the individual school's own resources. In spite of many employers' beliefs to the contrary, it is customary to practise school leavers in application form-filling and interview techniques as well as provide a first-hand impression of local work places.

It can be seen that many of these facets are dependent for realism and immediacy upon the co-operation and provision of access by employers and others in the local community. Where these courses appear to be most successful then degree of involvement in and support by the local community is a determining factor. Often these carefully structured curricula are supplemented by a network of contacts for work experience. The subsequent contact between individual pupils and employers can lead to the offer of a job and accounts for the much remarked phenomenon that those with mild mental handicaps who have been provided for separately at school often fare better in difficult employment markets than the non-handicapped or below-average school leavers.

However, it has been noted that the almost universal increase in difficulties facing employers in the last two or three years has led to a reluctance - or inability - to provide placements for school pupils. Also the dramatic extension in many countries of special post-school work preparation and bridging courses referred to later has tended to squeeze out of the work place the pre-school leaver. Undoubtedly greater co-ordination between the two phases needs to be developed; for example if post-school work preparation courses are to become a permanent feature of provision for those who are handicapped - and the non-handicapped - in most countries, does the curriculum in school need to be quite so 'employment' oriented? What about the relative balance between the development of employment-related skills and knowledge and the aesthetic, physical, moral and social aspects of the curriculum? In some Member countries the content, and methodology, of courses at both the pre- and post-school leaving stage has appeared virtually identical, sometimes without an appreciation on the part of the respective teachers and course tutors that individual youngsters were covering very similar ground twice over.

Those with Severe and Multiple Handicaps

One of the main issues to emerge during the project is how this group is defined, particularly the upper borderline. Associated with this is the question of appropriate provision for them. Uncertainties are due to conflicts between ideals and realities which result in confused expectations. Whereas the objectives for those young people discussed in the previous section are clear, namely to enter employment and lead, albeit in some cases with support, the same kind of life as other citizens, objectives for those with profound handicaps are often more limited. Some, but by no means all, individuals may have very severe degrees of mental impairment, others however have such a mixture of physical disabilities, communication difficulties and learning problems that the active mind behind them is hard to recognise and the individuals concerned find adequate expression immensely difficult. For all with severe and multiple handicaps, appropriate educational programmes from an early age are crucial. The development of these programmes and their implementation is indicative that more progress towards autonomy and a satisfactory life can be achieved than was at one time supposed.

One of the essential aspects of provision is that the pattern of daily life should be as normal as possible. This normalisation principle, now widely accepted, has implications for where education takes place. It is with respect to this group that integrative practices vary most widely from country to country. In parts of Italy there is the presumption - and the practice - that even those with the most severe disabilities should be educated in mainstream classes of schools. The same is true in some parts of the United States, at least to the extent of special programmes which take place in mainstream schools. Elsewhere it is this group that most often remain in day and boarding special schools or receive their education in schools in hospitals or social institutions.

It is clear that placements in mainstream schools requires great understanding and tolerance on the part of teachers, non-teaching staff and parents and close collaboration with other professions. It remains an open question whether this strategy is in the best interests of all concerned. Few would now dispute that placements in isolated institutions should be avoided, but the debate between special schools and provision within ordinary schools is much more finely balanced in relation to the most severely disabled.

Wherever education takes place it is more often a genuinely co-ordinated multi-disciplinary approach with priority given to social competence and communication skills. Vocational training and preparation for adult life is less generalised with the development of specific motor skills and training for particular work being given more prominence.

Nevertheless, for the majority, work may not be a realistic option after school and this of itself provides substantial difficulties in curriculum building. Often activities in and around school centre on what would be regarded in other contexts as peripheral leisure activities, days out to places of interest, the seaside, the country, the shops, horse-riding, swimming and the like. Thus emphasis is on the provision of a happy environment and experience as much as preparation for the future, although the hope, no doubt, is that the latter will flow from the former.

Those with Physical and Sensory Disabilities

The thrust towards integration has, in recent years, been most obvious in respect of those with physical and sensory disabilities who are not severely or multiply handicapped. This has been particularly true where children have shown intellectual ability and need rigorous academic courses. Progress has been dependent on adequate supporting services such as health care and therapies for the physically disabled, interpretation of language support for the hearing impaired, and brailling and other resources for the visually impaired. Results have been promising in the early school years, but as specialist subject teaching and academic demands increase there are often pressures on scarce supporting resources and, as already mentioned, some difficulties in providing specific preparation for transition for small groups in ordinary schools. These problems have led to greater emphasis on separate preparation courses immediately after the school period. But in some countries opportunities for those young people who are not academically able but have no serious learning difficulties are often limited and not sufficiently demanding.

It has been the practice in a number of countries to provide very specific training during the last years of schooling for a varied range of occupations that have become associated with particular disabilities, for example massage and acupuncture for the blind in Japan. But the young people and their families are seeking a much wider range of employment possibilities

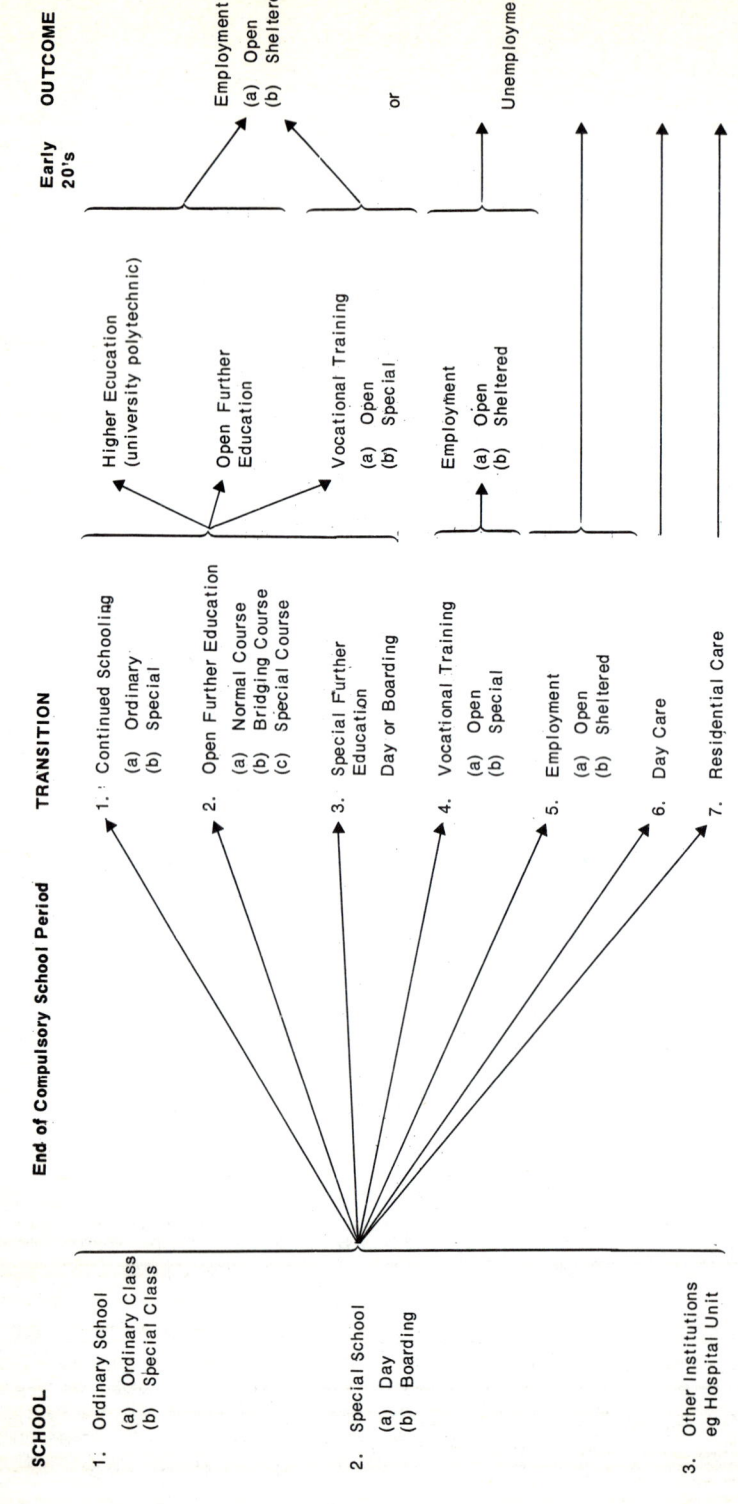

Figure 1 STAGES IN TRANSITION

and this has had an effect on preparation at the end of the school period.

Transition

It has already been noted that the age at which those who are handicapped leave full-time education varies considerably from country to country and obviously between individuals in the same country. In Scandinavia, attendance at high school or college is overwhelmingly the norm at 18 or even 21 years of age. Recent legislation in the United States lays upon education authorities the duty to draft an educational and training programme for every young person receiving special education up to and beyond 21 years of age. Elsewhere, even in countries with relatively sophisticated provision below school-leaving age, such as the United Kingdom, opportunities beyond 16 years of age are much more restricted and haphazard and only recently has access to further education and training come to be seen as a right. Clearly those countries (such as Spain and Portugal) where general full-time education to 16 years of age is not automatic for all have relatively limited provision beyond this stage except for the more intellectually able who may gain places at the universities.

Thus the options facing the young disabled school leaver vary widely in their scope (see Figure 1). Some may be able to remain at their school, or transfer to another school for an additional year or years of full-time education; this opportunity may be particularly critical for those suffering from mental handicap, but whose intellectual development may be accelerating at the normal leaving age, or for those who are particularly emotionally immature for whatever reason. Further education via a placement on a mainstream full-time college course will normally be restricted to the intellectually more able whose disability is physical, although even here severe practical difficulties can be encountered. The most dramatic growth in recent years has been in the availability of special work preparation courses, usually college-based. Some are designed specifically for the disabled, such as the French and United Kingdom examples described later, others for any school leavers at risk of long-term unemployment, an increase in which has been the common stimulant in the development of those courses.

However, most young people who are handicapped, often a higher proportion than in the population generally, will be seeking full-time employment at the end of compulsory school. Those with severe handicaps are likely to be guided towards sheltered employment or day centres some of which provide training such as adult training centres in the United Kingdom. Those who succeed in getting a job may also accept a commitment to off-the-job part-time training in those countries where that tradition is strong. But much more commonly the disabled in employment are likely to receive no additional general education or significant vocational training after leaving school. Finally some of those who are handicapped, and not by any means always the most severely disabled, will find themselves unemployed, often without even the amelioration of special bridging courses aimed at vocational preparation. The evidence in most countries is that this group is increasing disproportionately to the rest of the population.

Assessment and Careers Counselling

The range of opportunities facing most young people who are handicapped on leaving school has increased in complexity in most developed countries, either because the pattern of possible continuing education and training has become more comprehensive or because the range of possible employment has increased. However, the risk of unemployment is acknowledged universally to be greater, so that the complex decisions which face them may be limited by lack of genuine choice. But while work remains the major objective of transition from school, it is not surprising that the teachers are very conscious of their responsibility to prepare young people who are handicapped for the world of work.

We have seen earlier that work experience is often an integral part of the school curriculum as indeed is careers education in the wider sense. The extent to which education and training at the school level ought properly to be job-specific is a common issue and often hotly debated. It may well be that enhanced levels of unemployment will lead to a task-oriented approach to vocational education in schools - learning to operate a cash till rather than about the retail trade generally.

Bearing all these considerations in mind it is therefore important that parents and young people should have adequate guidance and counselling at all stages of transition, starting when individual programmes for the final years of schooling are planned. Such guidance and counselling should be based on adequate procedures for multi-disciplinary assessment of the individual and knowledge of the range of possibilities. In Yugoslavia, for example, the team customarily consists of a doctor, who is a specialist in educational medicine, another doctor with a knowledge of industry, a psychologist, a special educator ('defectologist') and a social worker, usually trying to achieve a close co-operation with the parent. Elsewhere teams may be different and include other professions. In the United Kingdom the specialist careers officer makes a major contribution, working with schools and employers to discover job opportunities.

Assessment is at its most effective when inextricably bound up with curriculum planning; the pupil's response to the curriculum, his relative successes and failures, are fundamental to the process of assessment and equally an assessment of current abilities and disabilities should determine curriculum design henceforth. The work of Hobbs and others in the United States rests on classification for employment being undertaken not on the basis of handicap but of services required in order to gain employment and remain productive.

A stimulus to more rational assessment of disabled young people has been the growth of the 'right to work' movement in many countries. In Norway it is axiomatic that everyone has this right in the same sense that the franchise is universal. Achieving meaningful employment for all is of course another matter. Until recently a generally held view in New Zealand was that the 'breadwinners' needed permanent employment and if this was achieved then social and economic policy was successful; employment for others was simply a bonus. Now employment is seen much more as the right of all; married women, the socially and educationally deprived, ethnic minorities - and the disabled.

So the imperative placed upon the multi-disciplinary groups, the teachers or the careers counsellors, whoever is eventually responsible for placement, is in all countries to maximise the employability of the disabled, by identification at the earliest stage of latent skills, careful advice and preparation for job application. Needless to say the general raising of expectations in this way, paralleled as it is in most countries with a shrinkage in job opportunities, can create considerable tensions and consequently an increasing tendency to consider alternatives to work. Nevertheless most disabled school leavers will want a job, either immediately or after further training. In order to help them, the key requirements are likely to be:

a) effective and early assessment of individual potential;
b) improved job requirement analysis - often employers have an erroneous concept of the knowledge and skills required to perform a particular job within their own organisation;
c) more pre-employment preparation for the work place;
d) for the more severely disabled, more sheltered employment opportunities.

All these require a careers or vocational guidance service - whatever its title - with adequate numbers of staff specialising in the particular needs of the disabled. Responsibility at national government level for this function sometimes sits rather uneasily between labour market and education ministries, as for example in New Zealand and the United Kingdom. However, the crucial test is whether the practitioners 'on the ground' are able to co-operate - teacher with careers counsellor, medical practitioner, psychologist or social worker - so as to identify the individual pupil's strengths, build on them and compensate for his disadvantages.

Work Preparation Courses

It has already been remarked that both in special schools and ordinary secondary schools there is considerable - and increasing - emphasis directed towards preparing for the work place and sometimes even the imparting of job specific skills such as typing or animal husbandry. However, it is at the post-school stage that the most marked development of special courses has occurred in the last five years. Experience in Japan, and through work with the severely handicapped centred on the University of Oregon, suggests that whereas those with mild or moderate disabilities may more appropriately be given a general preparation, the severely disabled benefit most from specific training for a defined work placement. However, there is some evidence that latterly courses for the former group have come to be directed at particular job opportunities, no doubt under the pressure of increased competition for available jobs. The achievement of balance in educational provision between the specific, which limits breadth of opportunity, and the general, which may dissipate energies of teacher and taught alike, is a quest common to all curriculum builders whether pre- or post-school leaving.

Over the whole range of disabilities the same social trends and aspirations which have promoted integration in education are producing a greater awareness of the need to prepare for access to open employment. The traditional pattern of separate vocational training for a limited range of occupations, or even a single 'reserved' occupation, piano-tuning for the blind in Western Europe or acupuncture (until it became very profitable) in Japan, is rapidly being changed by the growth of vocational education and training in ordinary colleges. This growth goes hand in hand with a more thorough identification on the labour market of those occupations that young people with handicaps can perform effectively.

However, the maze of options is often hard to penetrate even when the disabled youngster has opted for work preceded by training rather than more full-time general education or sheltered employment. Responsibilities for sponsoring and running special courses are often shared by national, regional or local education authorities, health, social welfare and employment and manpower planning services. Sometimes there is a significant contribution from voluntary organisations.

Consequently a first essential to effective service delivery is that young people and their families should have complete information as to what is available in their area or on a residential basis.

The scope and objectives - and the length - of special preparatory courses at the post-school stage vary considerably between countries, and within the same country. Often the courses are open-ended with students leaving whenever they obtain a suitable job. In Australia, for example, the Commonwealth Department of Social Security has established two work preparation centres for slow learning and mildly handicapped adolescents. The centres are equipped for light manufacture but also provide social competence, training and functional academic skills. Work training aims at establishing good work habits and job performance skills. The environment is deliberately industrial with work sub-contracted by private firms. The staff are a mix of tradesmen, social workers, vocational counsellors and teachers, and the co-ordinator is a psychologist. Recruitment can take place at any time between 15 and 19 years of age but the intending student must recently have left full-time education. Referrals can be made by schools, social workers, employment agencies or parents and selection follows an orientation programme at the Centre. The students receive a special cash grant equivalent to the current level of unemployment benefit, except those under 16 who receive a smaller grant. The Centre judges when they have reached open employment standard and then helps them find a job - in other words the course has no fixed term but is geared to individual progress and attainment. The Centre maintains a watching brief once open employment has been secured. In some cases it becomes evident that the student will not be ready for open employment in the foreseeable future and a transfer to sheltered employment is usually arranged.

At North Nottinghamshire College of Further Education, and elsewhere in the United Kingdom, similar provision is made to that of the Australian centres although this time in a setting which is fundamentally educational rather than industrial. Nevertheless there is a purpose-built workshop and a high level of co-ordination with potential local employers. Another distinguishing feature is that, as well as the specially designed and separate courses for those with hearing and visual disabilities and moderate physical and mental handicap, support is given to disabled students attending normal college courses leading to recognised qualifications and advanced study. In addition special bridging courses are provided to enable disabled school leavers subsequently to take normal courses. Between 1970 and 1980 the college's ability to provide for the disabled has grown from 10 student places to between

150 and 200 and this is by no means untypical of expansion in many countries.

In Norway and other Scandinavian countries, courses at the post-16 stage tend to be more lengthy, in line with the more universal pattern of full-time education for the non-handicapped to at least 19 years of age. Hence the Birkelid residential school for children with learning difficulties and moderate mental retardation, as well as catering for 7- to 16-year-olds, has a programme of further education for the 16- to 19-year-olds.

Work training in the first year of this three-year course starts in the school workshops and in the laundry and other service areas of the school. It is seen as a diagnostic period to assess the student's skills in relation to job opportunities in his home area. During the second year up to three days per week are spent in a public or private company with at least three placements for each student during the course of a year. The third year continues the combination of work and school but full-time work placements are made as opportunities occur. The student lives independently in a room or flat and is encouraged to manage his own shopping, cooking, budgeting and leisure time. Sixty to seventy training places are available in small private companies and service industries and these opportunities are of course fundamental to the success of the scheme. Recently the generally worsening employment situation in many countries, including Norway, has made for even greater difficulties in securing short-term work experience placements for the handicapped. It is likely that this factor, more than any other, will act as a brake upon the extension of schemes such as this one and the others referred to which are, by common consent, invaluable in smoothing the transition from education to work.

Potential Employers

So far we have concentrated on the preparation of the potential employee; however, he is entirely dependent for his opportunity to work upon the identification of a sympathetic employer prepared to give him his chance. We have seen in Chapter I that the world-wide recession has intensified the pressures upon employers not only in the private, but also the public sectors, to seek ever greater productivity. Labour costs are an increasingly significant proportion of total costs in almost all spheres of activity; consequently even the well-disposed employer may find it more and more difficult to accept a disabled youngster who may be able to undertake the tasks required but at a slower rate.

From an employer's point of view the degree of handicap can be of prime importance; he must avoid either placing an employee in a hazardous situation or creating a bottleneck in production. As the President of the New Zealand Employers' Federation said recently, .."any contribution that employers can make may only benefit the few who can keep up with the almost remorseless requirements of industry".

Nevertheless in all countries there is not only a substantial number of employers who judge the disabled applicant solely upon his ability to do the job but there are many who are prepared to make some allowance in terms of speed of completing tasks and therefore productivity, whether or not disablement employment quotas happen to be operative.

The closer relationship between those responsible for educating the disabled and potential employers, particularly as a result of vocational orientation of curricula in the later school years, and post-school work preparation courses, are undoubtedly the most productive way of enabling the disabled to gain a foothold in open employment. The work of specialist careers counsellors as well as teachers in building these relationships and ensuring that employers understand what the education world is trying to do, as well as giving teachers generally an insight and experience of the world of work, is crucial.

The Family and Personal Development

During growth through adolescence, all young people are particularly vulnerable to feelings of inadequacy and insecurity as they seek a sense of their own identity and develop a capacity for personal autonomy. This process can be enhanced by appropriate education, family support and above all by successful participation with others in work and recreation. Those with disabilities and significant difficulties may be additionally handicapped during the phase of personal development if opportunities are not afforded to discuss and come to terms with their disabilities, to make a realistic appraisal of future prospects and to help them participate as fully as possible in a range of community and social activities. The parents of these young people may need help in encouraging independence and accepting reasonable risks after years of protective care. Transition to work is often only effective where young people are helped to develop realistic job and social aspirations and to extend to a maximum their capacity for independent living.

In both these respects the role of parents and the family can be crucial. Often in the past, professionals responsible for providing services for the disabled have planned not only educational and medical programmes but also the future social circumstances of their clients; not because of a deliberate rejection of the importance of the family but because of an estimation that the personal inadequacies of parents in particular make it necessary for others to take over their normal role. More recently it has come to be appreciated that even parents of limited abilities play a key part in the personal development of their disabled children. Consequently it is now more the rule than the exception for parents to be involved in the multi-disciplinary consideration of appropriate provision for their children. In the United States, for example, recent federal legislation lays a duty upon all education authorities to agree an individual programme with the parent not only at the school stage but also in relation to preparation for employment, job seeking and further education. Nevertheless, status as true partners still remains to be accorded to parents by many professionals.

A consideration of the future lifestyle of young people who are handicapped is crucial in planning transition. Many may continue to live at home or return home permanently from residential education. Those with severe handicaps, whether going out to open or sheltered employment, or attending day centres, may continue to make demands on parents long after others of the same age have left home. The position of parents is discussed in detail in the paper by Mittler, Cheseldine and McConachie later in this volume. This also mentions an example from Nebraska of sheltered, small groups living away from the family. There are a number of similar developments in other countries to provide a normalised semi-independent lifestyle which have their implications for education and training programmes during transition. Those less severely handicapped may increasingly opt for independent living at a relatively early age as has become more common among their contemporaries. Clearly these considerations are as vital as choices between open and sheltered employment, continued education and day care and inextricably interwoven one with the other and should be reflected in education and training programmes.

The World of Work

The movement towards a greater degree of integration at the school stage has been paralleled in most countries by a determined effort in recent years to provide as normal a life as possible after school. Fundamental to this is, of course, provision of a job and preferably one alongside the non-handicapped. In some countries this desirable goal is enshrined in legislation: Sections 503 and 504 of the United States

Rehabilitation Act of 1973 are intended to provide the basis for integrated community-based services available to all the disabled as a means of maximising independent living and access to open employment. In the United Kingdom the recent Warnock Report opts unequivocally for the normalisation of living and working opportunities and has been accepted in principle by Government. These general positions are paralleled by governments in all Scandinavian countries whatever the distinction of detailed policy and the same is true in most other countries. Also there is now a greater awareness of the desirability of these goals in the population generally; newspapers and radio and television programmes highlight and espouse the cause of integration at work as did, for example, both the Wall Street Journal and the Manchester Guardian in March 1979. The International Year of the Disabled in 1981 provided a further opportunity to heighten public awareness of issues relating to employment of the handicapped.

A further spur is the increasing recognition of the considerable cost of maintaining the disabled in unproductive capacities. Social Security benefits vary considerably as between countries, but universally the funding of disability and unemployment benefits plus the cost of support services are a not inconsiderable part of total social welfare budgets. In the Netherlands, for example, the unemployed disabled receive from the Government 80 per cent of previous earnings or, if they have never been employed, a grant dependent upon their degree of disability, both of which are indexed to rises in the cost of living; in no circumstances is the guaranteed income from the state allowed to fall below the minimum legal wage (net).

Thus the thrust towards normalisation on humanitarian grounds is increasingly supported by a hard-headed calculation of the social cost of unemployment.

Open Employment

As we have noted in Chapter I, there is a fundamental disagreement as to whether disablement quotas, whereby governments require or induce employers to make up a proportion of their workforce from those on a disablement register, are useful. In the United States, for instance, 'affirmative action' must be taken in this direction by firms with Federal Government contracts of more than $2,500, including provision of 'reasonable accommodation'; experience in the United Kingdom and elsewhere is historically that many handicapped have been given jobs, particularly in the public sector, which they might not have been offered in the absence of some kind of requirement.

However, individuals and rights groups often resent the stigma of special registration and consider that a categorisation as 'different' and as an 'obligation' which the firm has to carry militates against genuine integration.

On the other hand explicit governmental policies towards the employment of the disabled, as in Italy, appear to be generally welcomed. These policies are easiest to realise in the public sector, where recruitment can be controlled directly by central or local government. A recent survey throughout the United States by the President's Committee for the handicapped showed that the vast majority of local authorities had positive policies and often a written action plan. For example in Burbank, California the authorities have committed themselves publicly to:

1. Remove architectural barriers to the employment of the disabled.
2. Maintain job check-lists identifying matching abilities.
3. Ensure that the disabilities of those to be employed must be 'stable' and any illnesses non-communicable (no doubt a valuable reassurance to potential work-mates and management).
4. Check that the qualifications for the job held by the disabled match those of non-handicapped people in similar jobs.
5. Insist that departmental managers make themselves familiar with employees' particular abilities and special needs.

The emphasis here, whilst enabling, is also that the disabled must be able to hold their own with the rest of the workforce, although the principles do not exclude the possibility of a lower level of productivity.

The City Government in Philadelphia has appointed a Project Co-ordinator who is himself handicapped and who conducts detailed interviews with disabled job applicants concentrating on the identification of their abilities rather than disabilities. It is generally accepted that those with handicaps may need a more thorough induction programme; the Wisconsin Civil Service, for example, provide special on-the-job training for 94 entrants per annum with a wide range of disabilities after which they take their place within the normal workforce. They are paid the standard minimum wage from the outset.

Modification of the Working Environment

In the public sector also it may be easier to achieve necessary physical modifications to the working environment. The private employer can often face the possibility, or certainty, of lower productivity, allied to standard wage rates for his disabled employees; it is then asking a great deal of him to invest in what can be fairly substantial capital items. In any case the provision of curb cuts, ramps, wide doors for wheelchairs, modified door knobs, special toilet facilities or telephone dialling aids are all much easier of realisation if considered when buildings are first designed. In all countries there is inevitably a gigantic backlog of necessary modifications to buildings both in the public and private sector. However, much can be done via the provision of portable metal ramps, the designation of special parking bays, the introduction of speech recording and other micro-technology and so on.

Income Levels

It has already been remarked that positive recruitment policies are easier of achievement in the public sector - although here too demands for increased productivity go hand in hand with manpower reductions currently. But particularly in the first months of employment the handicapped may simply be unable to justify their place as an 'economic unit of production'. In Norway, to try to counter this disincentive, the first two years' wages can be paid by the Department of Mental Health. The work experience courses already described and common to many countries normally involve a payment of a wage by the state while the disabled are operating on employers' premises, or a continuation of unemployment benefit. Thus for the employer any contribution made by the disabled is a bonus which he does not have to fund in the early stages.

However, when an employer decides to place a disabled person in a permanent job, whether after a special induction period or not, he has to consider not only the firm's financial interests but also frequently the financial interests of at least part of his work force. Often workers in manufacturing industry, and increasingly in other jobs, will be paid a wage calculated at least in part on the basis of their productivity or performance. Consequently, they or their trade union speaking for them may be, at best, lukewarm about the recruitment of someone who may jeopardize maximum productivity and therefore bonuses.

Thus, whilst practically all industries can provide some appropriate opportunities for the disabled - truck loading, making cartons, welding, retail selling or whatever - the attitude of fellow workers, as well as potential employers, can be crucial. In Parma, Italy, for example, considerable success has been achieved in placing young people with Downs syndrome in public sector jobs; but despite a clearly defined government policy, private firms have been much more reluctant to follow suit.

Predictably the greatest achievements appear to be where those responsible for educating, training and counselling the disabled make determined efforts to pave the way with potential employers and workmates. The concept of the 'named person' proposed by the United Kingdom Warnock Report, but not accepted by the Government, can be particularly valuable in this respect. The named person may be social worker, teacher, careers counsellor or any one of a number of professionals responsible for supporting the disabled, and the choice should be made by the multi-disciplinary group as seems most appropriate in each particular case. There is thus one person who is the initial reference point who can seek out potential job placements, accompany the disabled person to interviews and also talk to possible workmates. In Scandinavia the identification of one sympathetic supporter for the disabled amongst the work force, not necessarily or even perhaps usually, the supervisor, has been found to be efficacious. In Sweden Adjustment Groups of employers, employees and members of the Labour Market Board have also been shown to make a positive contribution within places of employment to creating job opportunities for the occupationally handicapped.

Just as the disabled are becoming more organised and articulate collectively within the community, so there are signs that the forwarding of their special interests in the work place is being sought. In Germany, for example, since 1974 handicapped workers in many industries elect their own representatives at enterprise level to works or staff councils. The law now requires that this opportunity must be provided in all establishments with a minimum of five substantially disabled workers. Whether this helps to promote integration or normalisation is, of course, debatable.

Sheltered Employment

Here, there are two broad categories, but with considerable overlapping and duality of purpose in many workshops. There are those workshops, centres or industrial enclaves which aim to provide extended employment on as near as possible an economic basis. Secondly, there are those establishments wholly or primarily concerned with relatively short-term training and preparation with the objective of preparing for open employment. The former must have a close concern with marketing and financial control, the latter will place a much heavier emphasis upon training and social welfare support with relatively minor, or perhaps no financial return from sales. Bellamy's paper demonstrates the high degree of investment of time, imagination and skill training required in edging the severely disabled from sheltered to open employment.

Clearly much provision involves a combination of the two functions and one factor is almost universally apparent whether the objective is extended sheltered employment or short-term preparation for open employment. That is the inadequacy of available places whether residential or at day centres. This has been exacerbated recently in many countries by the growth of unemployment among the more mildly handicapped. This presents those responsible for placement with the dilemma whether to allocate sheltered opportunities to this group who are likely to be more productive in the longer term and also have a greater chance of securing open employment after training, or to continue to reserve available places for the severely handicapped.

This problem is paralleled by an increasing difficulty in securing work which can be undertaken in the centres. Manufacturing industry is often now operating below capacity and therefore more reluctant to make or continue agency arrangements with sheltered workshops. At the same time those workshops which manufacture directly for the open market have been hit at least as hard as other manufacturers by the world-wide recession.

Such work as is available is often boring and repetitive and it may be that these difficulties will encourage sheltered workshops to increase the liberal, educational and also recreational elements in their programmes. In other words there will be a shift of emphasis away from the economic productive units towards centres providing for the needs of those attending - or resident - in a more comprehensive way. Even those centres that concentrate exclusively on production can often only afford to pay wages much below the accepted rate in the surrounding community. In 1976 the average throughout the United States was only half the national minimum wage. In other countries payments are seen much more as 'welfare' rather than 'wages'.

One of the most encouraging development of recent years has been that of 'half-way houses' between sheltered and open employment sometimes under the aegis of a University Department as in Oregon or as an enclave within a normal industrial enterprise and subsidised by local or central government.

The Communita di Capodarco in Rome has 170 residents 20 per cent of whom are disabled. The Communita is self-managing and occupies a row of apartment houses indistinguishable from other flats. There is a central rehabilitation centre and a vocational workshop which maintains close links with a local engineering factory. In early 1979, five severely handicapped young people were under training as mechanics. A Downs syndrome youngster was acting as caretaker. A co-operative was producing both electronic equipment and ceramics. The independence of the group and of individuals within the group was impressive but a subsidy from public funds will usually be required for this kind of enterprise.

Recently attention has been focused on enhancing the participation of the disabled in voluntary work and socially useful activity; it has been remarked that in most developed countries there is no shortage of work, only of resources to pay for it to be done. Two years ago the Warnock Report stated that in the United Kingdom 'few handicapped people are engaged in helping other handicapped people ... with the shortage of social and welfare workers of all kinds there should be plenty of scope for handicapped people to give encouragement and unpaid help to others who are facing problems they themselves have had to overcome.'

Obviously such an approach pre-supposes a reasonable disability pension or other income from the state. It is important too that equal encouragement to voluntary work for the unemployed is given both to those who are handicapped and those who are not.

Part Two

REVIEWS OF SOME TRANSITION PROGRAMMES

I. THE YEARS OF SCHOOLING AND TRANSITION TO WORK IN THE DEPARTEMENT DE L'ORNE, FRANCE

By C. Grey
Education Officer, Somerset Local Education Department, England

The purpose of the visit was to study provisions made in the Département de l'Orne to ease the transition of the handicapped adolescent from the world of school to the responsibilities of adulthood and working life. I concentrated, therefore, on that part of the special education service that provides for the needs of handicapped young people in the age range 12-16.

The Département de l'Orne is the southernmost of the three départements which make up the area known as Lower Normandy. It has a population in the region of 500,000 and its principal town and administrative centre, Alençon, is relatively prosperous thanks to the generally healthy agricultural economy of the region it serves. Discounting tourism, farming and related enterprises, food processing and packing are the major wealth creating industries. There are few giant national or multinational concerns offering large-scale employment to school leavers - but the many small firms, often still family businesses, provide a rich variety of opportunities albeit on an irregular and ad hoc basis. Indeed, it may be due precisely to this combination of small employers in a predominantly rural and, therefore, almost by definition, more caring society that unemployment problems appear to be less critical in the Orne than in more industrialised parts of the country.

SPECIAL EDUCATION IN THE ORNE: THE GENERAL PICTURE

Because private initiative has been responsible for the origination of much of the special education provision which exists in France today, it was not subject before 1975 to the same degree of centralised control as the mainstream education system. In that year, however, an obligation was placed on all local authorities (Law

No. 75-534) to adopt a corporate approach towards special education provision by establishing Departmental Commissions to be responsible for developing a co-ordinated pattern of care for handicapped people "from cradle to the grave".

According to the official list, the Académie de Caen (the three Départements of Manche, Calvados and Orne) has 109 establishments specialising in the education, training and welfare of the handicapped. Of these 29 are in the Orne and carry as many as 15 different designations. All establishments catering for the age range 0-18 are today the responsibility (both in terms of funding and management) of either the Ministry of Education or the Ministry of Health and cater for the whole gamut of handicaps, physical and mental including maladjusted youngsters. The establishments make provision for thirteen categories of handicap as follows:

> blind; partially sighted; deaf, partially hearing; non-mobile, brain damaged; non-mobile physically handicapped; other physical handicaps; three categories of ESN - mild, fairly severe and very severe; social problems; behavioural problems; psychiatric disorders.

The Commissions just referred to were established in May 1976. The C.D.E.S. (Commission départementale d'éducation spéciale) is responsible for the placement of all handicapped children and adolescents from birth until they assume the responsibilities of adulthood or, if too severely handicapped to live a normal life, 20 years of age. Another Commission, the CO.T.O.RE.P (Commission technique d'orientation et de reclassement professionnel) looks after the needs of those older adolescents (from the age of 18) and adults who, by virtue of the degree of handicap suffered, require further vocational training or permanent therapy. The latter Commission is jointly administered by local officials of the Ministries of Health and Employment while the C.D.E.S. operates under the aegis of the Local Education Authority (Académie) and the Department of Social and Health Services (Département d'actions sanitaires et sociales - D.A.S.S.).

THE WORK OF THE C.D.E.S.

The 12 members of the C.D.E.S. are representatives of the Académie(3), the D.A.S.S.(3), funding agencies(3), private special education establishments(1) and parents' support groups such as A.D.A.P.E.I.(2). Members serve for a term of 3 years and the presidency of the Commission alternates on a yearly basis between the Chief

Education Officer (L'inspecteur d'Académie) and the Departmental Director of Social and Health Services. The secretarial support is provided by a member of the Chief Education Officer's staff, the deputy secretary being a member of the staff of D.A.S.S.

The Commission basically performs three tasks. Firstly it is responsible for nominating the establishments or services providing special education corresponding to the needs of the handicapped child or adolescent while having a duty to stress, in accordance with the spirit of the law, the priority to be given to finding the means to integrate handicapped youngsters into normal schools. Secondly, it has to determine if the degree of handicap is such that placement in a special education establishment is the most appropriate solution. Finally, it has a responsibility to determine entitlement to a Carte d'invalidité (C.I.) which confers certain financial benefits on the handicapped person's family. The C.D.E.S. may and does, however, delegate some of its powers to two other smaller specialised groups known as Commissions de Circonscription, one of which takes a special interest in the problems of handicapped children aged 3-12 (C.C.P.E.) and the other orientated towards the needs of 12-18-year-olds (C.C.S.D.).

The C.D.E.S. normally meets once a month and I was invited to attend one of its sessions.

The documentation on each case before it had been prepared for the meeting by the Secretary as a result of the deliberations of the Commission's professional advisory committee (équipe technique) comprising a special education teacher, an instructor, a psychologist, social worker, school doctor, child psychiatrist, medical adviser and representatives of spending agencies. One member of the Committee expanded orally on the summary that had been tabled giving such details as age, domicile, place in family, family background, academic, social, psychological, medical details including the results of tests administered on the child concerned and concluded by stating the Committee's recommendations.

In several instances discussion of the case was followed by an interview with the parents whose right it is to attend the meeting of the Commission when their child's case is to be considered. Where parents have expressed a wish to be so involved, an opportunity is given for them, also, to visit the various establishments under the aegis of the C.D.E.S. that can offer the required programme and facilities. It seemed that the Advisory Committee's recommendations are designed to coincide as closely as possible with parents' wishes, though it was stressed that in the last analysis it was up to the parents to decide what was best. At the same time great care was taken to ensure that all the specialists were in agreement too before the placement was finally confirmed. Some parents were reminded, however, that they could in no way abrogate their responsibilities and that they were expected to do what they could from within their own resources, financial and physical.

During the course of the morning's meeting some twenty cases were considered. They included severe social problems resulting from rejection by parents; psychotic delinquency; behavioural problems; severe learning difficulties; autistics; orphans with emotional problems; congenital disorders; physical handicaps; disablement due to accident. The age range of the subjects of the cases was 2-20. Some cases remained unresolved for one reason or another and were, therefore, referred to one of the two sub-committees of the C.D.E.S., the C.C.P.E. or C.C.S.D. in the case of nursery and school age children or to CO.T.O.RE.P. in the case of older adolescents. Where problems arose, for instance over transport for handicapped youngsters to and from home at weekends, the Commission gave assurances that every possibility would be explored. Sources of funding to help in such instances appeared legion.

PROVISION FOR THE HANDICAPPED ADOLESCENT:
FIVE ESTABLISHMENTS DESCRIBED

As indicated elsewhere there is an enormous variety of special education institutions serving the needs of the handicapped adolescent in the Orne. Visits were paid to seven institutions, five of which catered at least in part for handicapped youngsters in the age range 12-16. A brief description, albeit impressionistic, of these five will perhaps convey something of the nature of the provision made.

Institut pour infirmes Moteurs-Cérébraux (I.M.C.)
La Ferrière aux Etangs

Situated in the small and isolated community of La Ferrière aux Etangs, once a centre for iron ore mining, in the middle of beautiful, thickly wooded countryside about 60 km. west of Alençon, this privately established and maintained I.M.C. has places for 24 boys and girls aged from 3-16 with varying degrees of mental handicap from fairly to very severe and, therefore, having mobility problems. About half the children live within easy travelling distance (15-20 km.) of Ferrière aux Etangs and are, therefore, able to return home to their families at night. The remainder, however, live too far away to travel daily between home and school and arrangements are made for these children to be fostered locally from Monday to Friday.

The school, which is open 210 days a year, is housed in a collection of buildings once belonging to the mining company and has had a good deal of internal alteration and redecoration carried out. In addition to a number of more or less conventional spaces decorated and equipped as appropriate to the particular age group and handicaps catered for there is a good-sized gymnasium specially equipped to help youngsters with specific handicaps. There is also a small therapeutic swimming pool and a comprehensive range of domestic and sanitary facilities. Outside, workshops provide an opportunity for youngsters to improve motor co-ordination and there are open-air spaces including a small vegetable garden at the disposal of the pupils.

La Ferrière aux Etangs has call upon 26 staff of whom 15 are full-time, 5 half-time and 6 part-time. The full-time staff is, in addition to the Head, 2 professional "éducateurs" or instructors, 2 trainee assistants, 4 ancillary assistants, 1 physiotherapist, 1 nurse, 1 cook. A psychologist and 2 doctors attend as required.

The establishment is funded by the Ministry of Health on the basis of "prix de journée" which is a figure calculated by dividing the global cost of running the school by the number of places available and paid to the establishment each week depending on the actual number of places taken up each day. Inevitably, as the Head lamented, such an erratic method of funding leads to all manner of budgeting and accounting difficulties, not to mention the need constantly to redeploy or lay off staff depending on the number of children on the books. It is really just as well that in a rural area such as this there are not the opportunities for alternative regular employment.

The unexceptionable general aim of the establishment is to help children to achieve, commensurate with the degree of handicap suffered and the individual's potential, the greatest possible level of independence in the intellectual, physical and social spheres in order to facilitate their integration into society. The realisation of this aim, the Head indicated, depends on the total involvement, commitment and interaction of all the staff from Head and psychologist to drivers and kitchen assistants, not forgetting the parents and foster parents whose participation in the effort to ameliorate the children's conditions is regarded as crucial. The paedagogic training and therapeutic programme which the children follow aims to develop whatever intellectual, motor and social skills with which they are endowed, through exposure to as many different experiences as possible, both within and outside the institution and presenting them with challenging situations to reduce dependence and encourage initiative. The older children, the 12-16-year-olds, therefore, are given the opportunity to undertake all manner of practical activities including those of a domestic nature, gardening, odd jobs - for instance on the day of my visit decorating and assembling pot-plant holders - woodwork and pottery.

Very rarely, owing to the severity of the handicaps suffered by children placed at this school, are 16-year-olds able to proceed from here to a more or less normal life or, as the prospectus puts it, "socio-professional milieu". The majority enter some kind of protected work environment, either an "atelier protégé" (sheltered workshop) or a C.A.T. (Centre d'aide par le travail) described in detail in Martin Davies' paper, following. Sometimes, if it is considered in their interests, 16-year-olds return to their families. This is especially the case with youngsters from farming backgrounds when light, unskilled employment on and around the farm is not difficult to arrange.

There is no doubt that La Ferrière aux Etangs is a very caring, humane, establishment which achieves through the dedication of its staff, support of parents and with but a limited budget some quite remarkable results enabling children who otherwise might have remained little more than vegetables to live a useful albeit limited, in terms of opportunity, working life. The devotion of the Head and his wife - who acts as an ancillary assistant - is total, and few people could possess a better understanding of the problems faced not only by the handicapped child but also by his parents having as they do, a severely mentally handicapped child themselves. There are, I was assured, many similar establishments in the Orne achieving comparable results.

L'Ecole Nationale de Perfectionnement (E.N.P.) de la Ferté Macé

Still called unkindly by some of the local inhabitants "The Mad School", the E.N.P. in La Ferté Macé is housed in functional, modern, purpose-built accommodation on the outskirts of this typical little country town about 50 km. north-west of Alençon. Since 1951, 80 Ecoles Nationales de Perfectionnement have been established all over France to take youngsters from the age of 12 until 16/17 whose level of educational retardation is described as mild (an I.Q. range according to the Wechsler Intelligence Scale for Children test of 65-80 was quoted). Of the 80 E.N.Ps in existence at the moment, all but a handful are single-sex establishments; only 10 cater for girls. The boys, it seems, are more difficult to contain in the normal school situation than girls.

The E.N.P. in La Ferté Macé received its first pupils in September 1976 and now has on roll 150 boys all of whom have been referred by the C.C.S.D., many on grounds of behavioural difficulties, and come from all over the Orne, with some from neighbouring Départements. The girls from this area are catered for in an E.N.P. at Dinan, near St. Malo in Brittany. Placement at an E.N.P. rather than at one of the Sections d'Education Spécialisée (S.E.S.) usually attached to secondary schools in major towns is determined by reference to geographical, socio-cultural and scholastic considerations as well as the state of inter-personal relationships in the adolescent's family. 120 of the boys are boarders but the school insists that every weekend or at least every other weekend, boarders return home or go to foster parents in the vicinity. Transport costs are met by the Local Authority.

The accommodation gave an impression of spaciousness, if slightly austere in character, and the state of the fabric bore witness to the building's capacity to house so many potentially boisterous youngsters both in terms of its durability and design. No doubt it also has something to do with the kind of regime adopted by the school. Besides general classrooms and the facilities one would expect in a boarding establishment, such as social areas and very large dormitories, there are extensive grounds providing excellent vocational training facilities.

Of the 53 adults employed at the school, the F/T staff includes 8 class teachers, 16 instructors in various skills including recreational activities, 4 craft workshop teachers, specialist technical drawing and P.E. teachers, and a nurse. The whole staff, teach- and non-teaching staff alike, the Head insisted to me, must regard themselves as being involved in a collaborative effort to ensure the boys' intellectual, moral and professional development. Above all, they must at all times set an example to the youngsters through a demonstration of their inter-dependence, sense of personal responsibility, commitment to their task and concern for their charges.

E.N.Ps are funded by the Ministry of Education and, in comparison with ordinary schools, are generously endowed. Parents' contributions are means tested so that the fees per term for a boarding pupil range from £3 - £87 equivalent. Day boys pay between £1.70 and £27. Since the E.N.P. is an establishment concerned with vocational training, parents are required to pay an apprenticeship tax, one third of which may be paid directly to the school itself either in cash or even in kind - workshop materials for instance - so that the tools and equipment can be more regularly up-dated to keep pace with technological advances.

The aims set out in the school's brochure refer to the development of the boys' intellectual, social and professional abilities so that on leaving the school they might better make the transition into the world of work and society in general. By virtue of being for the most part a boarding establishment, the school is able to lay great stress on the socio-educative aspect of the stated aims. Reference was continually made during my visit to the community spirit the staff try to foster, the encouragement of collective as well as individual responsibility and sense of duty, respect for others as well as self-respect, initiative, critical awareness and independence.

Lest the youngsters should believe, however, that the world of school is a mirror of the outside world. (which is not always as understanding of individual idiosyncracies as the school community) work experience plays an ever-increasing part in the pupils' programme as they advance up the school. On entry, at the age of 12 and until 14 years, pupils follow a course of basic education concentrating on Maths and French totalling 26 hours per week. From the age of 14, while their basic education continues concentrating on developing communication skills and always relating classroom study to practical activities, pupils begin a vocational training programme that occupies between 50 per cent and 60 per cent of their time in one of four areas; horticulture, building, carpentry and painting/decorating and glazing. At the end of six weeks, during which an opportunity has been given to experience all the different crafts, the pupil specialises in one, the choice having been made jointly by pupil, teacher and doctor. Since, however, all groups are comparable in terms of numbers (and the Head admitted that very little cognizance is taken of job opportunities available locally in the four trades) one cannot help wondering whether the "choice" of training course is not rather more directed than guided and whether that choice is necessarily in the best interests ultimately of the youngster concerned.

Having said that, however, the quality of the work produced or the record of it in each of the 4 areas is impressive. Certainly, as far as the older pupils are concerned most of the work is commissioned by outside customers to whose premises the youngster will often travel as a team member in one of the school's minibuses to work on site. As pupils near leaving age the school makes arrangements for them at least to visit and, if possible, work for local employers, on 3-week to 1-month work experience placements. The school is justly proud of its record in succeeding to break down prejudices of local employers, many of whom have been happy to offer permanent employment to youngsters graduating from the E.N.P., so well trained have they been.

During the course of their career at the E.N.P., pupils' progress is constantly monitored both subjectively by staff and more objectively by medical and psychiatric staff. From the moment of entry, a comprehensive record is maintained on every aspect of the pupil's performance in class, in the gymnasium, in the workshop, behaviour both in school and out. From an examination of this at regular fortnightly meetings the "équipe éducative" decides in consultation with the family what medical, therapeutic, physical or educative treatment is necessary in the child's interests.

It would be wrong to describe the E.N.P. at La Ferté Macé as a school for the maladjusted although a number of youngsters are admitted because they cannot be contained in a normal school situation. The success of the E.N.Ps - my impression was firmly that they are very highly regarded - seems to be in their unashamed concentration on vocational training and basic skills related to that training the relevance of which to their life after school is immediately obvious to otherwise potentially maladjusted youngsters.

Sections d'Education Specialisée

Similar provision to that offered by the E.N.Ps is found in special education units attached to secondary day schools in the larger towns. I was able to pay short visits to both the schools in Alençon having units, the C.E.S. (Collège d'enseignement secondaire) Racine and the C.E.S. Balzac, which between them serve the needs of Alençon and the immediate vicinity. Racine and Balzac are similar in size each having approximately 900 boys and girls aged between 12 and 16 years. Their special units receive children of both sexes in more or less equal numbers at any age from 12 onwards. The 125 youngsters on roll in each unit are categorised as mildly sub-normal i.e. having an I.Q. of between 60 and 85 on the locally applied scale.

The Special Education Unit is physically an integral part of the school but has exclusive use of purpose-built accommodation set aside for its activities. In addition to general classrooms, there are generous and well equipped "workshop" facilities and other specialist rooms. While the Headmaster has overall responsibility for the organisation and administration of the Unit, there is a specialist team of teachers in the charge of a senior member of staff. The pupil/teacher ratio for classroom subjects is 1:16 and in practical subjects, no more than 1:8.

As at an E.N.P., between the ages of 12 and 14 years, pupils follow a course of basic education concentrating on the development of communication and numerical skills. At the age of 14 both boys and girls spend half their time (13 hours per week) developing practical skills in one of the Unit's four training workshops - two for boys and two for girls. It is interesting, however, that the nature of activities undertaken by the boys - building, including painting and decorating, glazing, tiling etc. and metalwork - is much more strongly career orientated than those offered to the girls - dressmaking and home sciences. This apparent inequality of opportunity reflects, I was told, the state of the job market, at least as far as handicapped youngsters are concerned, where girls experience much more difficulty in finding employment than the boys, the majority of whom, thanks to work experience schemes in their last year at school, are absorbed into the building industry and allied trades. As far as the girls are concerned, the aim of the curriculum is basically to prepare them to undertake the responsibilities of running a home and manage the domestic economy. Nevertheless, a number are able to make use of the skills they acquire in handling, for instance, industrial sewing machines and large capacity laundering equipment in local dressmaking houses and in the hotel trade.

Although I can only bear witness to the practical aspects of the students' work - my impression was that the quality of the work, both in the classrooms and the workshops, being undertaken by youngsters in all areas was generally high. After preliminary training in the use of tools and equipment, the staff try to ensure that the work the youngsters undertake is not just "exercices de poubelle" to be consigned upon completion to the dustbin, but, as far as possible, real tasks carried out to real specifications, in short "for real".

At the C.E.S. Racine, boys on the building course had laid concrete paths between blocks, built storage sheds and had entirely redecorated the interior of the Section, whose bright colour scheme, if a little riotous, gives an air of gaiety to otherwise austere corridors and stairways. At Balzac one group of boys were engaged upon the building of mahogany bookcases for a member of the main school staff while another group proudly exhibited their current project to convert another member of staff's minibus into a mobile home to take him and his family round the world! These particular undertakings were, I was told, typical of the "real" jobs upon which the boys were for the most part occupied.

Such commissioned work is paid for at the rate of 4 francs an hour plus the cost of materials, the income accruing being used for the benefit of the Unit and School in general. During the last year 1978/79, income from commissions amounted to 17,000 F at C.E.S. Racine and 15,000 F at C.E.S. Balzac. The scheme has, it seems, the support and co-operation of the Trades Unions and is backed by the law. (It is a matter of speculation, however, as to what the attitude of skilled workmen in the area might be towards the scheme if there were severe unemployment amongst them). Each Unit has and maintains its own minibus which is used to transport pupils to outside jobs at clients' premises.

It is, I was told, much more difficult to attract commissions that would employ the girls' skills although some income is made by the sale around the school of the results of their baking and expenditure saved by the operation of an in-house laundry service. The motivation of all the youngsters I met seemed high and, I was told, discipline problems amongst the group, many of whom have a high potential for disruption, are as a consequence, minimal.

The staff evidently all work very hard to ensure that the young people in the Units have as few problems as possible when they leave school either by helping them secure a permanent job to go to or by arranging enrolment on a further 6-9 months training course at a Centre de Formation Professionel des Adultes, for which they are paid 600 F a month at age 17 and 1600 F after the age of 18. Follow-up of the Units' graduates have shown a high level of successful continuing employment.

Institut Médico-Pédagogique et Professionel "La Garenne"

The I.M.P/I.M.Pro. "La Garenne" which is one of five such establishments serving the Orne, lies no more than 5 km. from Alençon in a thickly wooded area known as Saint-Germain-du Corbeis. The beautifully landscaped campus has been carved out of the surrounding woodland and covers 12 hectares. Although described as modern and functional, the buildings and their layout reflect the care that was taken in the design to present a non-threatening aspect. Indeed, it is clear that when constructed in 1971, no expense was spared to provide welcoming and comfortable boarding, classroom, workshop and administrative accommodation. It was originally financed jointly by national, regional and departmental agencies responsible for health and welfare and, although today firmly part of the Département's special education provision, it remains under the aegis of the Ministry of Health. It is administered locally, however, by the Director of the Caisse d'allocations familiales (C.A.F.) de l'Orne, the Department of Health and Social Security, in close liaison with the Social Services Department.

"La Garenne" has places for 96 boys and girls aged between 6 and 18 years, all but 16 of whom are boarders. Places are allocated in the normal way through the C.D.E.S. or one of its Commissions de Circonscription to youngsters who are categorised as mildly E.S.N. but exhibiting personality and/or emotional problems which may also have resulted in behavioural difficulties either at home or in the ordinary school situation. The age of admission varies depending obviously on the point at which problems begin to manifest themselves, successful diagnosis and the availability of places. While the latest age at which a youngster may be admitted is 12 or exceptionally 14, the majority enter the school at 7 or 8. It is not necessarily expected, however, that having once been placed at an I.N.P., a child will spend the rest of his or her school career there. There is always the possibility of being admitted as a day pupil to a special unit attached to a C.E.S. such as those I visited at the Racine and Balzac Schools. On average, I was told, youngsters remain at "La Garenne" five years with those of secondary school age on admission normally graduating at the age of 16/17. Between 10 per and 15 per cent of those admitted whose problems prove more intractable pass to the responsibility of the CO.T.O.RE.P, at the age of 18 and are placed in a suitable training or therapeutic establishment.

As I have already implied, the visitor is immediately struck by the interesting arrangement of the buildings and pathways, the combination of functional simplicity and tasteful landscaping so that one's immediate impression is of a well-ordered yet friendly environment, a not unimportant consideration in the treatment of maladjusted youngsters. The School is especially well provided for in terms of accommodation and facilities of all kinds. There are eight boarding houses, the internal organisation of which is described below, workshops for boys' and girls' crafts training, greenhouses and large vegetable garden, all the produce of which helps to supply the school kitchen, a gymnasium, all-weather pitch playing field with running track and other athletics facilities, a number of indoor leisure and club rooms. In all areas, furnishings and equipment were of good quality and in a good state of repair reflecting the school's firm stance on individual and collective responsibility.

The adult/child ratio at "La Garenne" is generous by any standards. All told 75 adults are employed in a variety of capacities; there are 40 "éducateurs" about half of whom are responsible as house mothers and fathers for the children's general welfare and all non-timetabled activities outside normal school hours. A great deal of emphasis is placed on the role of these pastoral staff in the process of socialization or "rééducation" to which, certainly in the early stages of a child's placement, the formal educative programme is subordinated. The importance of the part played by all non-teaching and ancillary staff - cleaners, gardeners, drivers etc. - is not overlooked, however. The Headmaster was insistent that these adults have an equally crucial role in the disturbed child's rehabilitation and that a teamwork approach is, therefore, essential. The school enjoys the services of a substantial cadre of medical and paramedical staff including generalist doctors, psychiatrists, psychologists, physiotherapists, nurses and medical ancillaries, whose presence as part of the establishment's staff reflects the necessity of and importance placed on the "medical" treatment of pupils in the overall response to the problems exhibited by the youngsters on entrance and throughout their stay.

The "prix de journée" fixed for "La Garenne" is not inconsiderable F.280 (or close on £30 sterling at the current exchange rate) a contribution towards which is paid by parents on a sliding scale. The high per capita cost is not to be wondered at, however, given the generous scale of staffing, buildings and equipment.

As indicated elsewhere, all pupils at the school including the day pupils are allocated to a "pavillon" or hostel, of which there are eight on the campus. Youngsters are placed according to their age on entry to maintain a balance of ages within each pavillon's family group. Over each group of 12 youngsters preside 3 house parents (either 2 men and 1 woman or vice versa) whose responsibility it is to organise where necessary and supervise the children's activities at all times when they are not in classrooms or workshops. All meals are taken in the pavillons and domestic chores are performed by the youngsters according to age and ability. At all times during the day and night a member of staff is within easy call of any pupil, which helps promote a feeling of security which so many of the children attending the school are said to need. In short, the pastoral staff try to provide the sort of loving, caring and yet structural environment which a good family home would try to provide. From what I saw of the children, staff and the cosy interiors of the four-bedded bedrooms I have no reason to think that in this respect at any rate, their aim was not being achieved.

Between the ages of 6-14, all but about a dozen youngsters whose psychiatric disorders are so severe that a normal educational diet is considered totally inappropriate and is replaced largely by therapeutic activities, follow a scholastic programme which concentrates on the basic skills of reading, number work and drawing which it is hoped will equip them the better to undertake both the leisure time activities they are encouraged to pursue and workshop tasks later in their school career, when they graduate from the I.M.P. to the I.M.Pro. at 14. The children are divided by a combination of age and ability into 4 classes of 12 pupils each being in the charge of a specialist teacher and trained assistant. The pedagogic approach adopted by the teachers I had the opportunity of observing was highly individualised and appeared to capitalize on pupils' immediate interests and responses to stimuli. There was evidence of a good deal of home-made equipment and materials designed to answer specific needs of single pupils.

After the age of 14, if they are considered mature enough intellectually and socially, the adolescent youngsters embark upon a training programme which envisages approximately 50 per cent of the time being spent on workshop type activities while a related academic programme occupies the other 50 per cent. As in other establishments visited, craft facilities for boys were much more impressive and extensive than for girls who, as elsewhere, have to be satisfied with domestic subjects. The boys on the other hand enjoy the facilities of a large workshop devoted to trades required in the building industry including joinery, painting and decorating, glazing and wrought-iron work. A great deal of space is given over to the horticulture section which has the use of two extensive greenhouses for the cultivation of salad and other vegetables and house plants from which the school derives income. The standard of work and application to work which I observed in all practical areas was impressive. In some, youngsters who, I was told, were some of the most seriously disturbed, were working quite happily virtually unsupervised.

During the latter part of their time in the I.M.Pro. from age 15/16, every effort is made to give the young people concerned an opportunity of work experience, and the house staff in conjunction with the technical teachers must take great credit for the success they currently have in placing youngsters with local employers. At this stage, no wages are paid, of course, but in every other way the six-month placement is made as close as possible to the actual work situation. As elsewhere, placement on work experience schemes proves more difficult where girls are concerned, but I received the impression, I hope not unfairly, that the lack of opportunity for girls was of less concern for the head and his staff. Since boys outnumber girls at "La Garenne" by two to one anyway, the problem is quantitatively less significant but there appeared to be a general acceptance that girls could be adequately catered for back home on the farm with their families where helping with the household chores was the normal post-school prospect.

A comprehensive continuous assessment is made of all young people placed on work experience by both the receiving employer and the member of staff responsible for the placement in order that the school may try to remedy any deficiencies which manifest themselves in attitude, application, skills, etc. and so that ultimately any future employer may have as complete a profile of their potential employee as possible. One member of staff is responsible for securing the first job for youngsters leaving "La Garenne" and goes to great lengths to maintain contact with them, even helping to find alternative employment should the first job not work out. An indication of the school's success in placing its leavers was given me by the head in relation to the previous year's batch of 16- to 18-year-olds. Of the 15 leavers who remained in the Département - 11 boys and 4 girls - 13 returned to live with their families and (more important) of these 11 obtained, and had remained to date in normal employment. Those older adolescents who have greater difficulty in settling into a normal employment situation are given the opportunity of a further training course under the auspices of the F.P.A. (Formation professionelle pour adultes).

There is no doubt that the I.M.P./I.M.Pro. "La Garenne" is a successful institution responding to the needs of the large number of youngsters who pass through its doors not just effectively but in an entirely humane and caring way. The abiding impression one carries away is that thanks to the dedication and selflessness of the staff - as well, of course, as the high level of investment in the establishment in terms of staff and plant - the school manages superlatively to achieve its principal aim of equipping its pupils to play a useful and respected part in society.

CONCLUSION

In general it seemed that the provision made for these handicapped youngsters who are deemed employable is achieving a considerable degree of success although, in the context of a declining job market, it is debatable if it can be sustained. The success of the system lies, I believe, in the determined concentration on vocational preparation orientated towards specific trades but also in broader work experience terms, and the concentration in all establishments on basic academic skills directly related to that manual training. What impressed me especially was the extent to which the tasks undertaken by the youngsters in the age group 14-16+ were not just realistic but were actually real jobs which posed real problems to be solved, both in terms of technical skills to be mastered and social relationships to be formed to enable that job of work to be completed to the satisfaction of their clients. This establishes, at least as far as the handicapped adolescent is concerned, something that educationists generally have been reluctant to accept or perhaps even have a vested interest in not accepting, namely that in order to ensure the acquisition of social, work and life skills, the answer does not lie in devising a course of study about it but by giving the youngsters who are anxious to acquire such skills the opportunity of learning from their own experience with, of course, varying degrees of support and advice along the way from the "professionals".

II. WORK TRAINING IN THE DEPARTEMENT DE LA SOMME, NORTHERN FRANCE

by Martin Davies,
Senior Education Officer,
Buckinghamshire, England

This report concerns establishments in Picardy responsible for social and work training of handicapped adolescents and adults. Both establishments, one at Flixecourt, 20 kilometres northwest of Amiens, and the other at Petit-Camon, on the western outskirts of Amiens, are integrated IMPro-CATs. IMPro is an abbreviation of Institut Medico-Professionnel which serves the further education, social therapy and work preparation needs of handicapped adolescents aged fourteen to twenty. The CAT, or Centre d'aide par le travail, is a work training and occupational therapy centre for mentally handicapped adults over the age of twenty.

Since the end of the Second World War, IMPros and CATs have developed throughout France: there are more than one hundred in the province of Picardy, but the common pattern is for them to operate as separate institutions. This operation as an integrated unit is one interesting aspect of their operation; others include their evolution, management structure, day-to-day operation and practical and pedagogical approach.

Despite their proximity to Amiens, both establishments serve essentially rural areas of prosperous mixed farms and compact villages. The valleys of the Somme and its tributaries form an important market gardening area, with cattle rearing, cereals, sugar beet and fodder crops on the fertile rolling chalklands which characterise this part of Picardy. In the nearby towns, of which Amiens (150,000) is by far the largest, there has been a decline in the traditional textile industries, but a wide variety of new industries have come in to take their place, including food processing, engineering and chemicals. A large industrial estate has been developed in the last ten years between Amiens and Vignacourt. The region is very attractive to industry: it has easy access to the Channel ports and lies midway between Paris and the north-eastern coalfield around Lille.

This physical and economic setting is of considerable significance to those concerned with post-school provision for the handicapped. First, the combination of rich land and diverse industries has brought in recent years a relatively high level of prosperity and a low level of unemployment. Besides the obvious effect on job opportunities for young of all ranges of ability, this has also resulted in a generally sympathetic and co-operative attitude from employers and trade unions: vital for work experience schemes and industrial placements. Clearly though, the area, however attractive, is not immune from general national and international economic trends and the situation described above could deteriorate in the next year or two. Second, handicapped youngsters from country areas have advantages over their urban counterparts in that rural communities are commonly more tolerant and caring and farming families are more easily able to occupy such youngsters at home.

PROVISIONS WITHIN THE EDUCATION SYSTEM

In France, education is compulsory for children aged 6 to 16, but non-compulsory pre-school classes are available for children aged 2 to 5. At 11, pupils transfer to secondary schools and follow a four-year general course, increasingly in junior comprehensives known as collèges d'enseignement secondaire. At 15, they opt for a three-year examination course in a lycée, leading to the baccalauréat, or for shorter technical or vocational courses in a lycée d'enseignement professionnel.

For children with learning difficulties, there are special schools or special classes and units in ordinary schools. Special classes exist from infant school up to the end of the first cycle in the collèges. At 14 plus, those able to benefit from vocational training can be sent to an école nationale de perfectionnement or to a special department in a collège. The degree of learning difficulty is monitored by teams of educational psychologists who refer serious cases to a local advisory panel comprising guidance counsellors, doctors, social workers, psychologists and an inspecteur d'académie (the local adviser/administrator). This panel then advises on the most suitable teaching and where the children can find it.

The more severely handicapped and others with serious learning difficulties are referred to an IMP (Institut médico-pédagogique) which takes children aged 6 to 16 and is the main feeder to the IMPros. An interesting contrast with the English system emerges here:

IMPs, IMPros and CATs all fall under the auspices of the Ministry of Health. Thus, a child entering an IMP at 6 years of age follows a system which diverges sharply from mainstream provision and makes transfer back to an ordinary school progressively less likely. Nevertheless, and unlike the reaction in England in the early 1970s, this situation appears to be welcomed by most parents, psychologists and special educationists. The Ministry of Health is much less centralised than the Ministry of Education; it budgets on a regional basis and allows much more pedagogic freedom and local initiative. Despite the changes brought about in the mainstream system by the 1975 Education Act and the Haby Reform which began to take effect in 1977/78, it is still viewed with suspicion by many in special education as centrally controlled, inflexible and unsympathetic to individual needs.

The IMPros and CATs provide by far the most significant opportunities for mentally handicapped youngsters unable to find open employment. As in the United Kingdom, there are sheltered workshops, mainly for specific handicaps such as the blind, deaf or physically disabled, but otherwise provision is limited to hostels, psychiatric hospitals or staying at home.

THE IMPro-CATs AT FLIXECOURT AND PETIT CAMON (LES ALENCONS)

Origins and General Management Structure

In their external appearance, the IMPro-CATs of Flixecourt and Les Alençons are very different; Flixecourt opened just under two years ago in excellent purpose-built premises, while Les Alençons uses an old shabby country house, with a large garden and outbuildings, and has been in operation for more than six years. In their origins, management structure, number of young people, general philosophy and day-to-day operation, however, they have many similarities.

Each establishment was the result of local initiative in forming a Syndicat intercommunal, the overall managing body composed of two representatives from each of the communes served by the IMPro-CAT in question: 58 in the case of Flixecourt, 30 at Les Alençons. The Syndicat is the promoter of the scheme and the owner of the real estate, but delegates functional management responsibility to a Conseil d'administration, which is the employer. This council, or governing body, comprises eight representatives of the communes, elected by the Syndicat intercommunal: two parents; two officers of CREAI, the Centre régional pour l'enfance et l'adolescence inadaptées; and two representatives of the

Association des papillons blancs. (The latter is a voluntary organisation which promotes the welfare and support of the mentally handicapped and which itself runs a number of IMPs, IMPros and CATs.) The Directeur of the IMPro-CAT and officers of the Department of Social Security also serve on the Council but have no voting powers. The Président of the Syndicat is also Président of the Council.

The project at Flixecourt began with an inaugural meeting of interested parties called in February 1974 by the Papillons blancs and parents of mentally handicapped youngsters in the area. The particular concern was that, in the Département of la Somme, only the canton of Picquigny (the area north-west of Amiens towards Abbeville) had no post-16 provision for the mentally handicapped. Up to 16, the young people attended the IMP at Ailly-sur-Somme and a detailed census of pupils and former pupils had clearly demonstrated the need for the project. Those at the meeting included the local Senator, local and regional politicians, government officials and advisers, representatives of the communes, directors of other IMPros, headteachers and parents. Wholehearted support was given to the establishment of the IMPro-CAT, at an estimated cost of 3.4m francs.

The cost of the scheme was met by a grant of 40 per cent from the national government, a grant of 10 per cent from the Département of la Somme, an interest-free loan of 30 per cent from the Ministry of Social Security and a 20 per cent contribution, on loan, from the Syndicat intercommunal. The latter sum was achieved by a levy not exceeding 1F50 per inhabitant of the 58 communes.

Detailed planning was done by a research team comprising the Conseiller général of Picquigny, a psychiatrist, a psychologist, an architect of CREAI, four special educationists from the IMP at Ailly and two representatives of the Papillons blancs, with the power to co-opt expertise as necessary. The Syndicat was formally constituted in January 1975.

The site at Flixecourt was chosen because the village is one of the largest in the area, centrally situated and of relatively easy access, with all the communes within approximately fifteen kilometres. The spacious single story building was specially designed by the CREAI architect. The catchment area was fixed in liaison with the Syndicats intercommunaux at Doullens and Les Alençons.

Both Flixecourt and Les Alençons receive a state grant of 210F per person per day for the IMPro and 204F for the CAT and they are also allowed to charge for contract work undertaken in the community. The young adults in turn receive a salary of between 1000F and 1600F per month according to age, mainly in the form of social security payments, but pay back a daily charge, for means and materials, which meets about 20 per cent of costs. Payments do not relate to output or level of ability.

Both establishments operate a five-day, forty-hour week for forty-two weeks per year and staff and students share the same holidays. The teaching staff establishment is calculated on a 1700-hour year, with additional time allowed for meetings, preparation, staff development and absences and works out at a staff/student ratio approaching one to four. The general conditions of service are based on national recommendations in the Convention collective de l'enfance inadaptée of 1966, modified in 1973.

Flixecourt has a Directeur and eleven other teachers, plus a bursar, secretary, cook, driver and part-time cleaner. Part-time services are also provided by a psychologist, psychiatrist and social worker. At Les Alençons, the Directeur has twelve teachers, a secretary/bursar, a handyman/driver, two cooks and a part-time cleaner. He also receives services one and a half days per week from a psychologist and a psychiatrist.

The teaching staff are of two types, éducateurs specialisés and éducateurs techniques. The éducateurs specialisés are drawn mainly from the IMPs, though occasionally from work in psychiatric hospitals or penal institutions. They receive the same basic training as primary school teachers, followed by two years' teaching practice. They must then obtain a Certificate of Aptitude for teaching the maladjusted or the handicapped, which involves further academic study and teaching practice with children of the particular disability in which the teacher wishes to specialise. The éducateurs techniques are not qualified teachers as such but are craftsmen-instructors, specialised in a particular trade such as building, cookery or horticulture.

Flixecourt has a maximum complement of sixty. At present, there are 23 in the IMPro, with a maximum of 26 places, drawn exclusively from the IMP at Ailly-sur-Somme, and 30 in the CAT, with a maximum of 34. Les Alençons, which is full, has 30 in the IMPro, of which 25 came from the IMP at Bussy-les-Daours and the others by direct referral from ordinary schools, and 28 in the CAT. They take youngsters of both sexes, at any age from 14, whose degree of handicap is such that they could not reasonably expect to gain open employment without further training. The aim, therefore, is to further the development of each individual to increase personal skills, independence, social integration and employment potential, even if the extent to which this can be achieved is limited. Social and leisure activities are seen as an integral part of the programme and not merely as an annex to it.

Flixecourt's IMPro places are limited to young people of around 55 IQ and below, although they exclude seriously disturbed psychotics or medically unstable epileptics. There is a high proportion of mongols. Les Alençons has a much wider range of ability: at one end of the scale are profoundly mentally handicapped youngsters; at the other, adolescents of normal or just below average ability who are psychologically disturbed or maladjusted, but whose employment potential is quite high.

There are no non-ambulant cases in either institution. Entry to the CAT at 20 years of age is determined by an advisory panel of teachers, social workers and medical personnel and is initially on the basis of six months' observation, after which categorisation is confirmed for benefit purposes. There is no age limit in the CAT: at Flixecourt, the oldest worker was 37; at Les Alençons 29.

There are no residents. Most live with their families; about 10 per cent live in foster homes or social services hostels, and one youngster was on day release from the 2000-bed psychiatric hospital at Amiens. It is not uncommon to encounter serious social problems in the home situation, particularly in large families, and the staff of both establishments work very closely with parents in a supportive and counselling role.

Physical Facilities and Day-to-Day Operation

Day to day work is based on chantiers: work groups of approximately eight young people and two supervisors. The teams are of mixed ability and various ages and are drawn from both the IMPro and the CAT. The approach is essentially practical and there are opportunities to work both in the community and in institution-based workshops and other zones de travail.

The two IMPro-CATs offer similar opportunities, but in contrasting circumstances. Flixecourt occupies a spacious grassed site of 1300 square metres in fields and orchards on the very edge of the village. There is a small vegetable plot, but insufficient room for formal team games: this does not cause the Directeur any concern as he has no wish to 'institutionalise' the centre in any way. The very modern functional building is designed to give the best possible views over the valley, especially from the dining room and social areas, to encourage a feeling of 'well-being'.

The building has four main areas, an administrative block, a social/teaching area, a dining area and a workshop area. The social teaching area includes recreational facilities and the dining area a small flat for social and life skills activities. Workshops take up half the building and include areas for woodwork, metalwork, painting and decorating, sewing, horticulture and concrete work. A classroom adjacent to the main workshop is used for basic literacy and numeracy work associated with workshop activities and for art work.

The whole establishment has an air of civilised well-being, with no evidence of wilful damage and very little litter, and clearly concentrates on training rather than production. The workshops therefore are primarily skill centres: they offer opportunities to engage in a variety of activities with different materials, sometimes in a single article such as metal-framed, cloth-covered deck chairs with foam seats which were being made.

Les Alençons is much older: it makes use of a former private residence, about eighty years old, standing in two hectares of land alongside the main N29 highway and surrounded by a high wall. The garden has a large vegetable plot and animal and poultry enclosures and numerous outbuildings, with a caretaker's lodge.

Work on a new building to provide accommodation similar to Flixecourt will begin next year. The old building will be retained to provide additional social and practical areas with the upper floor converted for residential use, including accommodation for special residential projects for young people attending the centre.

All the basic building work on the new block will be undertaken by staff and students from the centre, with specialist services called in as necessary. The cost will be met by grants and loans: grants of 30 per cent from central government funds, 10 per cent from the Département, 10 per cent from the communes and 10 per cent from voluntary agencies and private donations; with a loan of 40 per cent from the state, repayable over twenty years.

Les Alençons and Flixecourt are very similar in their basic philosophies, with an emphasis on social training, informal education, developing a wide range of skills and integration into the community. There is clearly considerable freedom in approach, dependent on the views of the Directeurs and their staff, who see the whole way of life of their establishments as important. Thus, the programmes are carefully structured, but are not rigid or oppressive, and are made up of activities which are meaningful to the trainees concerned. They aim to encourage independence and self-motivation, rather than give specific job training.

At Les Alençons, the Directeur sees three fundamental concepts, 'being', 'doing' and 'learning', all built into a complex framework or web of relationships, expectations and motivations, and encouraged by a wide variety of situations. He aims to develop group consciousness and foster the particular relationship that can develop between a young person and a good teacher. He articulates three sorts of group within the institution: 'life groups', the basic synthesising group emerging from all the various day-to-day activities; 'workshop groups', giving not only a chance to learn skills and do something worthwhile but also social training, the chance to work with others in a disciplined situation; and 'large groups', when the whole establishment comes together, for example on an excursion or for the midday meal.

At the same time, the staff actively guard against an inward-looking institutionalising regime and parents demand marketable skills from the more able youngsters, particularly in the IMPro. The great challenge is to achieve a balance between the care and protection that handicapped youngsters require and the need to prepare them adequately for a place in the outside world. To these ends, great emphasis is placed on work in the community, through the medium of the chantiers.

Basically, the IMPro-CATs negotiate job contracts with clients, usually municipal authorities, small businesses or private individuals. An advantage to the client is that the work is usually less expensive than from a commercial contractor because the IMPro-CATs are exempt from TVA (value-added tax), but, of course, it is likely to take longer to complete and may not be quite up to professional standard. Most clients to whom I spoke, however, seemed to be motivated more by a desire to help integrate the young people in the community and broaden their experience. Neighbours showed curiousity on occasions, but no prejudice is encountered: indeed, the standard way of gaining new work is by personal recommendation of satisfied customers.

The two establishments differ markedly in the ease with which they are able to keep the chantiers occupied. Les Alençons, longer established and with better contacts, has no shortage of orders, while Flixecourt finds it difficult at the moment to find sufficient content or variety of work, particularly during the winter months when they have to resort mainly to the internal workshops. Part of the task of the staff is to scout for orders, although occasionally advertisements are also placed in the local press. They look particularly for jobs which offer a variety of tasks, preferably over several weeks, so that all the youngsters in a chantier can be usefully occupied, whatever their ability, and literacy, numeracy and other work at the institution can relate to the contract in a meaningful way.

Chantiers at Flixecourt are mainly involved with basic labouring. Jobs underway included digging and weeding in a market garden and in private gardens; laying and mowing lawns; laying paths for private householders and in the grounds of the IMP at Ailly; renovating cupboards and wardrobes; repairing municipal picnic tables and benches, and working in a riding stable. Forthcoming contracts were along similar lines and also included cleaning the river bed at Bettancourt, painting a balcony and fencing work.

At Les Alençons, the chantiers are organised more formally and some take on quite sophisticated tasks. The groups, though of mixed age and ability, tend to remain constant and form six specialist chantiers: building, joinery, catering, farm/garden, handicrafts and le groupe individualisé. This latter chantier is composed of the more profoundly handicapped and most difficult trainees and tends to remain within the institution. There are about a dozen young people in this category and they spend much of their time on basic social and life skills as well as working with the animals and in the garden. When they work outside the centre, they are sub-divided into small groups of three or four.

The catering chantier, all girls, has a permanent term-time contract to produce the midday meal four days per week for the village school at Vignacourt. The meals are produced at Les Alençons and transported to the school in special containers. The girls also prepare the IMPro-CAT's own lunches to a very satisfactory standard. Some of the foodstuffs are home produced; others they help buy from local markets and traders.

The masonry chantier has a full builders' licence and is fully occupied, with orders well in advance, including the new block at Les Alençons and a contract to build barns and stores on a nearby farm. Their current jobs at the time of my visit were the construction of retaining walls for gardens in a village about fifteen kilometres from the centre and, nearer home, the building of foundations for a partly factory-built house in another village. The village fifteen kilometres away is at about the economic limit in terms of transport costs and travelling time, but was clearly a good contract. The work they achieve is complicated and of a high standard; they are closely supervised, of course, with two skilled éducateurs techniques in charge, but it was interesting to observe how even the least able could be usefully occupied in digging, mixing, carrying, measuring and so on.

Both centres are well provided with trucks, vans and cars, eight in all, for transporting the youngsters and their equipment as well as providing car mechanics practice, and they also have motor coaches (shared, in the case of Les Alençons, with the IMP at Bussy-les-Daours). At the same time, youngsters able to use public transport are encouraged to do so as much as possible.

In both Flixecourt and Les Alençons, approximately 60 per cent of the trainees' time is spent on the chantiers. Of the remaining two days, one (Friday at Flixecourt, Monday and Friday mornings at Les Alençons) is devoted to sport and recreation, when the young people can opt for a wide variety of activities, all forming an integral part of the group therapy. They include art, pottery, woodwork, metalwork, music, table tennis, basketball, football, skating, swimming and horse-riding. The other day is given over to meetings, discussions and classwork, all specifically associated with current, forthcoming and completed contracts, with general policy and personal development. Each young person has a member of the teaching staff particularly responsible for his or her welfare and for monitoring progress.

Internal Management

Both establishments place great emphasis on teamwork and participation in general management, not simply by the Directeur and the teaching staff but by all the personnel and, as far as possible, by the young people themselves. This approach is also evident in the IMP at Bussy-les-Daours where my guides were the Directeur and the driver/handyman! The Directeurs see the whole staff as involved in the educative process; for the benefit of the young people, to foster the sense of community and to increase job satisfaction. This in turn makes the temperament and personality of all personnel of vital significance and helps to break away from traditional attitudes and relationships.

The management load is distributed, therefore, by means of formal and informal meetings and sub-committees. In some ways there seems to be an excessive number, yet the relaxed, informal and purposeful atmosphere of the two establishments suggests that the system works well.

The most important meeting hierarchically is that of the équipe technique. This is the main policy committee and comprises the Directeur, the psychologist, the psychiatrist, two éducateurs and one other member of staff. It meets for two hours twice a month. In addition, the whole staff meets for two hours once a week: on Wednesdays at Flixecourt and on Fridays at Les Alençons. Here the work of the various chantiers is discussed, reference is made to particular problems in respect of individual students or their home situations, and debates are held on general policy, financial matters and forward planning.

Once a week, for an hour, there is a management meeting between staff and student representatives and each chantier or workshop group elects a delegate. The week's programme is discussed and the young people put forward their ideas on how the jobs should be distributed, the composition of the chantiers and option groups, suitable contracts, and so on. Subsequently, time is set aside in the chantier programme for a Workshop Meeting, when the delegate can report to his comrades and, together with the éducateur in charge, receive reactions for the next session.

Individual staff, or small sub-committees of staff, take responsibility for such activities as the sports and recreation programme, use of the motor coach, course planning and finance. The staff, in fact, work a three session day, continuing for one or two hours after the young people have left at 16.00 or 16.15 and, during this time, as well as meetings and preparation, great importance is attached to liaison with parents.

Formal parents' meetings are held perhaps twice a year, but only about a third are actively involved: distance and transport are problems, particularly at Flixecourt. They are, however, encouraged to visit individually whenever they wish and the éducateurs specialisés have a regular programme of home visits, to discuss topics of social, educational and psychological interest. Sometimes they detach themselves from the chantiers, but usually go during the late afternoon session referred to above; they try to see each set of parents at least once a month. At Flixecourt, the secretary/bursar is also involved in this liaison work and gives advice on grants, subsidies and other financial matters. There is also close liaison with the feeder IMPs and with the parents of children who will eventually come to the IMPro. Opportunities are made for day release and visits by pupils in senior classes at the IMP.

CONCLUSION

It will have become apparent in reading this report that the IMPro-CATs of Flixecourt and Les Alençons have much to commend them as one method of dealing with the transition from school to adult life of handicapped adolescents. Reference has been made to the non-authoritarian, non-institutional régime, the purposeful and generally satisfying work experience, the sympathy and acceptance of the community and the involvement and dedication of the staff, who clearly put in many hours of work beyond the minimum. It is of credit to all concerned that the IMPro-CATs have had little difficulty recruiting and retaining suitable personnel, even on the craft and services side.

There are, however, two main impending problems as far as the teachers are concerned, one relating to open employment and work experience prospects, and the other stemming from the national <u>Loi d'orientation en faveur des personnes handicapées</u>, passed in June 1975.

In respect of the first, both Directeurs see as their main objectives education, preparation and, in some cases, rehabilitation for life in the outside world. Wherever possible, and particularly in the IMPro, this involves training for the ordinary job market or, failing that, for sheltered employment. In the short time that Flixecourt has been in operation, no young people have left either the IMPro or the CAT, but Les Alençons has an impressive record: since the centre opened six years ago, over half the intake has left for open employment. This may be partly because of the slightly more able complement that the establishment seems to have, but it is also a tribute to the work training programme and to the determination of the staff in pursuing suitable opportunities.

The general policy is to make direct contact with a sympathetic employer and arrange for an appropriate young person to attend the place of work for a trial period of three weeks or a month. No less than seven youngsters were working on trial at the time of my visit. One girl was working in a municipal day nursery; another in a café, and two others in restaurants. Of the boys, one was working in a joinery business, one at a Fiat garage and a third was with a large private bus company in Amiens. Taking the last case as an example, the company, Courriers Automobiles Picards, has more than two hundred vehicles and is able to offer a wide variety of work experience, for example on panel beating, painting, cleaning and renovation, and tyre work. The Managing Director was very sympathetic to the aims of the centre and had already employed a former trainee from Les Alençons for more than two years. The transport workers' union was also willing to co-operate; at present, there is no shortage of jobs at the more menial levels. The youngster on trial was a twenty-year-old from the CAT, of well below average intelligence, but a conscientious worker; the company was very pleased with his progress and the Directeur was confident that he would be taken on to the permanent staff. Besides transport and catering, other permanent open employment has been gained in shops and supermarkets, farming and horticulture and public services.

The potential problem referred to above could arise in two ways. First, employers and in particular the trades unions are likely to become much less sympathetic in the event of a declining employment situation. Second, and perhaps of more fundamental significance to the centres, because the CATs have no age limit but do have a strictly limited number of places, the effect of roughly half of each intake leaving for employment or for other opportunities is that gradually a larger and larger rump is built up of adults who have little prospect of any kind of gainful employment. This in turn could lead to the very kind of inward-looking dependent institutionalisation which the staff are so anxious to avoid.

The second potential problem, relating to the <u>Loi d'orientation</u> of 1975, is causing the staff of both institutions great concern and was referred to time and time again. The teachers' fear is that the edict will undermine the philosophical and pedagogic freedom which characterises the IMPro-CATs by requiring them, particularly the CATs, to concentrate too much on production, output targets and quasi-industrial activities. It is estimated that France has perhaps 3.3 million people who suffer from some degree of mental or physical handicap, of whom 1.2 million are under the age of twenty, and the aim of the law is to ensure that all of them receive the same rights and opportunities as other citizens. Unfortunately, it appears to see this in predominantly administrative and economic terms and recommends the creation of what many would consider to be a very divisive and cumbersome bureaucratic machinery. Under the revised system, benefits in the form of disability pay would relate to a person's work potential: thus, a person who was thought to have 80 per cent of the output capacity of an ordinary worker would have his payments reduced accordingly. Categorisation would be the task of a review panel known as <u>la Commission technique d'orientation et de déclassement professionnel</u> (COTOREP).

Clearly, this policy would require the CATs to re-orientate towards a production-conscious regime, where the social and life skills training would have to take a very subordinate position. The edict makes only the most fleeting reference to the social and cultural development of the handicapped. It also specifically excludes young offenders and the socially or culturally deprived and this could particularly affect an institution like Les Alençons, which has achieved the integration of youngsters with a wide range of ability and employment potential. Responsibility for the socially handicapped and for low achievers whose degree of mental handicap was relatively slight would pass to a much greater degree to the Ministry of Labour, which, again, the teachers view with suspicion because of apparent over-centralisation and inflexibility.

The Directeurs and staff of the IMPro-CATs hope that pressure from teachers, psychologists and others involved in the welfare of the handicapped, such as <u>les Papillons blancs</u> and <u>le Centre régional pour l'enfance et l'adolescence inadaptées</u> (CREAI), will be sufficient to result in a modification of the law, or at least greater discretion in its interpretation and sufficient flexibility to operate satisfactorily within it. Much of the criticism is very similar to that commonly directed against the Social Services' Adult Training Centres in the United Kingdom.

III. THE INTEGRATION OF PUPILS WITH SERIOUS LEARNING DIFFICULTIES INTO NORMAL WORKING LIFE IN NORWAY

by K.M. Helle
Work Research Institute, Norway

This paper is in two parts. The first describes the vocational preparation course provided in Birkelid School, a Norwegian special school, and the second a research project which looked at the response of those in working situations to the integration of pupils from Birkelid School. It has been edited for this publication.

BIRKELID SCHOOL

After little activity in the area of special education between the two World Wars, the Norwegian Parliament passed the Act of the Special Schools in 1951. This law made the state responsible for building special schools so that children with learning difficulties received relevant education. As a result of this law, Birkelid Special School - a residential school - was founded by the state in 1957 near Kristiansand with the task of giving special education to children with learning difficulties from the most southern part of Norway.

The school moved from an old, inconvenient building to a new and well planned school in 1971, with educational and residential accommodation for children and older students and the necessary service facilities. Birkelid had originally been a school for children aged 7-16; but with the move in 1971, the Department of Education decided that it should develop a curriculum for further education giving young students learning opportunities for at least three years (16-19).

The Special Schools Act of 1951 was abolished in 1976, and a new Education Act was passed, integrating the Special School Act. The new idea was to have only one Education Act embracing both special and ordinary education which were clearly defined as a responsibility of the local council authorities. At the same time a new Further Education Act was passed which placed responsibility for all further education on the county authorities.

As a result of this new legislation a great many of the state special schools were transferred to the local school councils. Birkelid School, however, is still run as a state school and is directly under the Norwegian Educational Department.

FACILITIES FOR FURTHER EDUCATION

The facilities for such education were rather inconvenient. One of the dormitories was in fact designed for older students with single rooms and common lounge, kitchen and bathrooms. Nor had the school building been designed with any workshops; there were only craft rooms for younger children. It was necessary, therefore, to rearrange the accommodation to provide workshops for wood- and metal-working. These restricted and temporary facilities made it necessary to find tasks outside the workshops and as a result the main kitchen, the laundry, the caretaker's house and the dormitories were used as training places. Additionally, places were sought in companies outside the school as a necessary and most important way to train students for a real job. Since it started the school has had contact with some 60-70 private companies.

THE CURRICULUM

The first five years from 1971 have to be looked upon as a trial and error period. With the initially inadequate facilities, the school had to try out different ways of arranging job training. After 5 years, however, it was possible to outline a curriculum.

The further education at Birkelid School consists of a period of three years, with the first year as a basic course, the second as the main training year and the third as a year of transfer to a more autonomous life of work and living.

In all the three years the main items in the curriculum aim at adjustment to society, e.g. the principal "rules" of society, civil rights and responsibilities, economics, social security. To these topics are added practical activities such as home economics, cooking, sewing, practical woodwork, repairs and various kinds of work training. Language and mathematics are also taught but in a way more individually related to the students' own interests and capacities.

The work training starts inside the school - in the workshops, in the laundry, in the dormitories or with other tasks on the school area. The first year is looked upon as a diagnostic year when it is ascertained what interests the students have, their dexterity, concentration, sociability, operational insight and so on. When these qualities are assessed, it is possible to decide what kinds of work are appropriate to start with. The aim is that training should be in a kind of work relevant to the student's home area; but in the more sparsely populated districts it is often difficult to find a suitable job for him when ultimately he gets home.

The next step in work training is to start in a specially provided job in a private or public company - for one day a week to begin with, and then two or three days a week if the student manages well. The working place should change two or three times during this external period.

The third year of training is a close follow-up from the second year, continuing with 2 or 3 days' work a week combined with school activities. Individually the students undertake a full working week when the right training place seems to be found. Together with the job training there is an independent living programme intended to give the students an idea of living on their own, say, in a flat.

For this programme, the school has hired some rooms in private houses near the school and students live on their own there for a fortnight or more, doing the shopping, managing their household accounts, choosing how to spend their leisure time, all by themselves. This is, of course, the most testing part of the programme. Those who are not earning their own money get a subvention from the school to cover food, other shopping, rent and leisure expenses. For students living outside school in this way an evening course has been arranged on "living on your own" which is followed up individually in the actual lodgings by the course instructor who has herself been a housewife. The staff of the dormitories also have a responsibility to follow up students living on their own.

STAFF

Together with the teachers, these colleagues - from the dormitories or course instructors - constitute a primary staff group which through their daily work and meetings between themselves continously care for the development of the students' training programme from the more basic items inside school to the more advanced stages when the students make their way into society.

Other personnel collaborate as a service group. These include a counsellor (who is also a teacher), a social worker, a psychologist, the medical staff and representation from the school's administration. The function of this group is to provide job training places, social security support, a testing and assessing programme and medical treatment. In all this, the counsellor is the most central person. In consultation with the others it is he who works out the job training programme for each student, looks for convenient places of work, and, with the social worker, arranges social security support. He is also very active in the work of re-establishing the students in their home districts.

The students

For the first couple of years, Birkelid got students from other special schools, some youngsters from mental hospitals and some who had been at home doing nothing in particular having finished school some years before.

The training programme designed was a very "open" one which would not suit a group of students with severe mental problems or marked physical disabilities. Nor was the school designed for giving treatment to the latter group, either.

We could characterise the present group of students by saying that they all have severe learning disabilities which could not be treated at any local school. Most students are ESN(M) but the picture of handicap is a very complex one. In addition to mental retardation a great many of the students have emotional and social disturbances which cause behaviour problems. A great many have minimal brain dysfunctions which impair co-ordination, cause concentration difficulties and hyperactivity. Some have physical abnormalities such as hearing losses, sight deficiencies or are slightly palsied.

A majority are socially deprived - children who have a lack of understanding caused by understimulation, social dysfunction, nervous problems because of severe family conflicts and lack of stability and emotional security. Thus most are multi-handicapped and require individually-based training and treatment.

Searching for training jobs

Some 60-70 companies are on the list of suitable training places. Most of these are in the private sector - small factories, workshops, petrol stations, stores, restaurants, hotels and shops. Some are in the public sector such as post offices, hospitals, council for the environment, or the state railways.

The counsellor who, as we have said, is the responsible member of staff, usually contacts the manager of the company and if he is responsive, the counsellor sees the workers who would be the mates of the trainee student. It is very important to get one of the working team to have a special relationship with him, to follow his progress and be a link between the work place and the school. The foreman, or his mates even, are given necessary background information about the student.

As soon as work training can start, the counsellor shows a direct interest, ensuring that the student gets the right bus, finds his way through the town and so on. He also gets information from the company as to appropriate complementary training that should be carried out at school. Companies prefer to confine their contact to a single counsellor.

Wages

We very soon realised that these young students, besides getting further education, were interested in earning money. From monies obtained through official rehabilitation schemes, labour authorities and social authorities, the school is able to provide wages for the students. These are often more like pocket-money than a realistic wage, but they are a great work stimulator. Some students, however, get higher wages of which they pay out a part for housing and food, while they are expected also to buy their own toilet articles and some clothes. Students living in their own accommodation have near normal wages and pay most of their expenses themselves.

The final stage

This phase of the training - culminating in finding a full-time job - is perhaps the most important. If the follow-up work is relaxed much of the previous training will have been useless. As we have seen, finding a suitable job in a suitable place is most important; so is somewhere to live if the student cannot be at home. A room in a private house with the owner looking after his special needs is the preferred solution.

The local authorities are asked to keep themselves aware of the special problems of the students as they leave the school - this means the social workers, social security staff, and the labour department. The Birkelid staff follow the student for a year after he has left to see that things go well, that he is not dropping out and that the local authorities are maintaining their interest. If necessary they can extend this follow-up work by a further six months. It has often been remarked that when the student is over 20 his maturity and independence develop more strongly.

THE BIRKELID RESEARCH PROJECT

In 1977 a co-operative project between Birkelid School and the Work Research Institutes was started to establish how the school's integration programme was working out in practice in the factories participating. Of special interest to the Work Research Institutes was how the factories were able to accommodate this integration within their normal work organisation. In more formal terms, the question set was: "Under what working conditions is the integration of handicapped workers in normal industry possible?"

In this project we departed from the traditional, individual approach in rehabilitation research. Instead of looking first at the individual's capacity for work, we concentrated on the capacity of the working place to integrate workers, with considerable differences in ability, in their normal operating procedures.

Methodological approach

The project should be regarded as a pilot study. We had no clear theories or hypothesis at the start and chose to work from personal observation and open interviews. Birkelid School has a register of the firms and factories with whom they maintain contact. From these we selected seventeen for our research so as to get as wide a variety of working places as possible (see Table 1).

Visits to the factories and other places selected took place in June and July 1977. They were mostly taken up with interviews with regular employees who had had the most direct contact with the integration work. Each interview pursued three main themes:

i) General information about the factory working conditions - problems and working environment.
 ii) Experience with the pupils from Birkelid School as workers in the factory - degree of satisfaction and problems.
iii) General evaluation of the integration work in the factory, suggestions for improvement and assessment of the need for such work.

Table 1

WORK PLACES SELECTED FOR OBSERVATION

Work places		Number of employees	Number of places so staffed
Food preserving industry	5	0 - 10	3
Mechanical industry	2	10 - 20	2
Timber industry	1	20 - 30	1
Warehouses	4	30 - 50	1
Construction	1	50 - 100	7
Service work	3	100 - 200	2
Farming	1	200 -	1
	17		17

Results

From our own observations and from the interviews, we got a convincing impression of enthusiasm for this kind of work among most of the employees in these places of work. For example, one interviewee said: "We rather find that it is positive for the general atmosphere here to have N.N. from Birkelid with us. It is interesting to find what he can do and it is challenging to try to make him feel comfortable and useful in the job". There seemed to be willingness to take on social responsibility in most of the work places, and one of the main conclusions of this project is that integration in normal industry is possible and may even be a positive experience for the other workers.

Table 2 shows how the employers/employees assess their own integration work.

Table 2

REACTIONS FROM THE 17 WORKPLACES

Assessment of pupil's work		Views on integration of the handicapped in business/industry	
Useful	9	Very good possibilities	4
Useful, but time-consuming	5	Good possibilities	10
Time-consuming only - not useful	3	Poor possibilities	3

Problems

The most common problems that arose in connection with integration of the Birkelid trainees were these:

For the employer: On the trainee's part:
Time-consuming instruction   Carelessness
Extra responsibility   Indiscipline
Extra control   Inattention
                              Frequent pauses in activity

We may put these problems into three main groups:

i) Time-consuming instruction and follow-up in the work situation.
ii) Lack of persistence in the work.
iii) Training in special abilities.

These findings are of importance in preparing training programmes for mentally handicapped young people. The main elements of the training ought to be fulfilling given tasks, ability to work for one hour with the same task without taking a rest, understanding instructions and doing what you are asked to do.

The actual jobs carried out by the handicapped workers in this research project were various. They included:

Washing
Finding things, bringing things, delivering them
Errands
Carrying things
Help in loading cars

Help in loading trucks
Clearing work
Sorting things (screws, nuts etc.)
Storage work
Normal production on the shop floor.

Often a job consisted of a combination of the tasks in this list. The problem is to organise them into a meaningful full day's work with a steady flow of operations to perform. In the factories where the handicapped workers take part in normal production the work is most often organised in small groups with job-rotation. Here integration is possible because the workers can decide among themselves what parts of the production line are suitable for the handicapped youngster. It is not necessary that he should manage all steps in the job-rotation chain.

Our studies naturally evoked a number of suggestions for improvements in integration programmes. The factories, for example, asked for qualified assistance in their instruction work. In teaching new tasks to the mentally handicapped, help from the teachers of the school or from specially trained instructors from the labour office would be valuable. There was a common experience in the places we studied that normal work is in many ways preferable to a sheltered job. Nevertheless, there are sometimes organisational problems in finding a suitable place for a mentally handicapped worker. In a normal job-run, and to solve this problem, sheltered jobs within the normal organisation may indeed be the answer. Sheltered jobs consist of tasks matched to the handicapped workers' abilities, they are outside the normal career structure and not open for non-handicapped workers. If there is measurable lack of efficiency on the job, part of the wage can be paid through social security channels (in Norway this is possible by contributions from the labour office during a training period or by a part disability pension).

From firms in the private sector we got the opinion that state-run concerns should greatly step up their programmes of integration and be more flexible in their employment routines.

THREE PLACES OF INTEGRATION CONTRASTED

A WAREHOUSE

If the warehouse is not too big and the storage system not too complicated, our informants judge this sort of place well suited for the integration of workers with learning handicaps. Carrying things, loading and clearing-up work can all be presented as natural parts of a working process. If the trainee could be given instruction in car or truck driving, this would be of the utmost importance in creating a meaningful and interesting job for him. A driving licence would help him a great deal in getting a normal job. The school has responded to this by offering special training courses for those wanting such a licence. The theoretical part calls for a lot of training time. (In Norway you must have a Class I driving licence before you can get an industrial truck-driving certificate.)

But in our study youngsters not able to drive a car have got work in transportation. They go with the lorries as drivers' mates, helping with loading and unloading. This may be made a useful and meaningful job, but our informants fear it will prove boring in the long run, so they stress the importance of the young men giving up the time necessary to get a driver's licence.

WORK IN THE SERVICE SECTOR

The service sector is the area of working life that has had, and predictably will have, the greatest growth in number of work places. It should, therefore, be of the greatest interest when integration work is being planned. Service work is highly differentiated, containing skilled, semi-skilled and unskilled jobs. In our study, it embraced service stations for automobiles and fuel, cafeterias and a social institution. For girls with learning handicaps it is most often in some kind of service work that integration is tried out.

We found that flexibility and the possibility of arranging tasks in new ways exist in service companies, and that integration of the handicapped has a fair chance of succeeding. There are, however, some special problems that are worth mentioning.

Contact with customers

Some of the pupils with learning handicaps living in a semi-sheltered school environment have personality or social problems. They may be too shy to cope with customers, or they may give wrong information. This is a serious matter for a service firm depending on the satisfaction of its customers. A customer coming to get some kind of service - say for his car or a meal - is not usually in an optimal state of tolerance. In Norway at least, what happens to your car is something you are very concerned about, and you are at your least tolerant over mistakes and being kept waiting. When you go to a cafeteria you are often tired and hungry, and even kindly people are not always at their best at such a time. The customer demands service, and the resulting contact with the customer in an integration phase may lead to problems for the handicapped worker, as well as for his employer.

In social institutions work with the patients is so demanding of tolerance and personal ability that you have no time left to take on integration work among your co-workers as well. It may be felt that extra time and extra effort should be used for the benefit of the patients, not used to integrate other members of staff.

If you take away the elements of customer contact and patient care from service work, the tasks left will consist of the most dull and uninteresting ones. Our informants were afraid, therefore, that integration in service work would lead to a situation where the handicapped workers were doing just such "back stage" work. They felt integration was possible, but these jobs must be made meaningful and given some sort of prestige.

As this is the sector where there may still be work enough in the future, it is important that we note, think through and solve these special problems.

FARMING

In this sector of working life there have been great changes in recent years. In earlier times, most integration of workers with learning handicaps took place here. Now, however, much of the heavy manual labour has been replaced by machinery, the farms are small and there are far fewer hired hands. It is possible that youngsters with learning handicaps coming from farming families will find some work to do on the land; but this will be in the family, not paid by anyone else. We have one example of integration in farming in our study: this took place during the harvesting season. At such a time this may always be possible; but apart from a family-owned farm, the handicapped worker will still find it very difficult to get a steady paid job for all the year round.

CONCLUSIONS

The principal factors that impress us as influencing the success of integration are the following:

1. <u>Integration must be part of the employer's personnel policy</u>

It is important that the company implications of integration work should be discussed seriously during the planning of the firm's personnel policy. A mere "be kind to the handicapped" attitude is not enough. Integration of the handicapped must be asserted as a desirable goal for the organisation as a whole and agreed upon therefore by all concerned. This means that any problems arising must be discussed at the level where integration will actually take place, as well as in the top management. The opinion of the trade unions also must be sought. It is predictable that such a procedure as this will encounter difficulties in times of widespread unemployment.

2. <u>The work group in which the integration takes place must be prepared to share responsibility for it</u>.

Important as it is to have some central body co-ordinating the integration programme, it is nevertheless on the shop floor that the training and actual social integration take place. Our observations show without doubt that the most crucial factors for success are the influence and tolerance of the trainee's work mates. It is therefore of the utmost importance that the integration operation be so organised that the working groups concerned participate in its preparation, in any changes in the work pattern that may be necessary, and in assessing its success or otherwise.

3. <u>Apprising co-workers of the trainee's personal handicaps</u>

Only if you are aware of the individual's problems can you meet them with understanding and tolerance. Relevant information about the kind of handicap and the deviation from normal efficiency to be expected, must, therefore, be given to the trainee's work mates. Some problems may arise because of prejudice against certain psychiatric or social disorders, so the personal information to be given must be discussed with the individual beforehand.

4. <u>Freedom on the shop floor to rearrange the work pattern</u>

The optimal arrangement of work tasks to suit the handicapped worker must be tried out in advance when change is necessary to create a meaningful job for him. Shop floor routines will be less disturbed if the changes affect one working group only, and if (as already said) the members of this group decide among themselves how best to work things out.

5. Sheltering the handicapped worker from normal efficiency demands and wage systems

Integration work will be made very difficult if the below-standard performance of one person influences the total wage for the other workers as may happen in some group bonus schemes. In such cases, ways must be found to segregate the work-handicapped from the normal wage system to protect his fellows. For his part, if his efficiency is measurably far below normal, special wages support from social security funds would be an appropriate way of providing a fair income and preventing feelings of injustice.

6. Rehabilitation expertise must be available

In a number of cases incomplete integration may lead to situations where professional assistance is called for. For example, information about financial support from social security funds may be needed; or the individual may want advice about alternative means of rehabilitation. Practical assistance in any crisis situation will always be helpful. We would therefore recommend that a contact person - whether from the school or the labour office - be appointed for each person still in the process of integration.

IV. THE INTEGRATION OF HANDICAPPED YOUTH IN ITALY

An Example in Rome: "CAPODARCO"

Dr. V. Bagnasco,
Servizio Minori Provincial di Parma

Abridgement of a report contributed to
the CERI project in 1979

The CAPODARCO centre is situated in an urban district of working class housing and slums in Rome in an area which has about 200,000 inhabitants. After years of neglect, new initiatives by local councils and social groups in the area are being taken to overcome social, health and educational problems.

Among promoters of these democratic initiatives was the Community of Capodarco which supported in particular the rights of citizens with handicaps to be integrated into schools, work and social life. Working closely with health and social services in accordance with reforms and new regional laws, the community responded by setting up a Rehabilitation Centre and a Professional Formation Centre.

In collaboration with employment initiatives and local communities the services of Capodarco have always aimed at the integration of those with handicaps into society. In the last few years the struggle has been to establish training apprenticeships in factories as well as stimulating the Workers Movement and Unions to accept the objectives of integrating those with handicaps into every factory.

There have been many tangible results of the centre's activities in the last three years. Many students with handicaps have been placed in jobs, others have increased their personal autonomy, socialisation and working skills. Above all, a type of intervention programme has been developed which can serve as a concrete model and qualified answer for meeting the needs of the adult who is handicapped which is integrated with social and health services and closely related to the normal training structures.

THE COMMUNITY OF CAPODARCO

The Community of Capodarco was founded at Christmas 1966 by ten people, all of them severely handicapped, in order to seek an answer to their own isolated condition. The small group was organised according to the principles of solidarity and of the participation of all in the management of the community. It accepted others with disabilities and developed its organisation so as to obtain recognition from the Ministry of Health as a Centre for Medico-social Recovery. At the same time a Centre for Vocational Training in electronics and ceramics was founded in Capodarco which was recognised by the Ministry of Labour.

The community was finally turned into a Moral Corporation in January 1971. From this first group other initiatives developed in various parts of Italy. Four small living and working communities were founded, a studying and living community and a centre for the recuperation of secondary and tertiary education. In 1971 a Centre for Research into the Integration of the Handicapped was founded in Rome to study the social integration of those with handicaps.

Through the activities of the Research Centre seven family groups and living communities were established, in District X and neighbouring districts, in which 70 people with handicaps live with others who are not handicapped with equal rights and responsibilities. These communities, which are fully integrated in their local neighbourhoods, have now become a point of reference for many people with handicaps in the city who are seeking solutions to their living problems.

In recent years the Capodarco Community has been engaged in a big sensitisation programme and in the organisation of demonstration services to stimulate local council initiatives. Among these are:

<u>The Centre for Physical and Functional Rehabilitation</u>. This is open to all citizens in the district, in particular to those with psychological and physical handicaps.

<u>The Centre for Professional Formation (Vocational Training)</u> which can accept up to 50 people who are psychologically or physically handicapped. It has been selected as one of 21 European Centres which are participating in the "First Programme for the Professional Readaptation of Invalids" adopted by the European Community in 1974.

<u>Working Co-operatives and Industrial Placement</u>. In co-operation with private firms, co-operatives were set

up that include 50 per cent who are not handicapped which work closely with normal co-operatives. Three main activities were articulated: industrial electronics, ceramics and horticulture/animal breeding. Which of these activities is emphasised depends on the economic characteristics of the district and local commercial possibilities.

TRAINING PROGRAMMES

In the first phase a heavy emphasis is placed on socialisation and autonomy, without neglecting professional activities, because the trainees come from a background of isolation. Progressive autonomy from the protection of the family and others is realised for some by coming to the centre unaccompanied on public transport, for others by taking a vacation away from their families and for yet others by making independent choices.

An attempt is made to develop the trainees' autonomy by making them face up to their individual problems. Cultural and expressive activities have made the development of awareness of problems easier and strengthened the conviction that they cannot leave every decision to parents, teachers and others.

A concrete way of developing individual autonomy is to keep trainees in constant contact with their neighbourhood through, for example, eating in restaurants, joining local festivities on May 1st. The aim of the programme is always a wider and freer range of encounters with others. This work has made it possible to carry out activities in an environment which is aware of and responsive to the integration of those with handicaps.

Some specific educational activities have been used to obtain these results:

Group discussion:

8-10 clients, co-ordinated by a teacher discuss a subject of common interest and work out a synthesis which is then hung out on posters.

Newspaper:

Through the class newspaper it was found possible to communicate one's own experiences to parents, companions, and neighbours.

Theatre:

Through texts written by the clients themselves, we have tried to develop verbal expression, control over gestures, reading and writing.

Discovery of the Environment:

This has contributed to the development of observational capacities, a critical understanding of problems, and establishing valid relationships with the neighbourhood.

Outings:

Outings to the Vatican Radio, the zoo, the racecourse, and working centres. Small outings with an instructor to buy materials.

Cineforum:

Discussions of films in small groups. The films have a didactic content intended to develop critical capacities.

On a strictly professional level we tried to create working situations that are very similar to a normal working environment in order to teach the clients actual production techniques. Practical work was emphasised, letting them discover the theory, unifying the three aspects of projection, realisation and verification. This was done in small groups.

After the vocational preparation, apprenticeship inside a factory enabled assessment of the client's capabilities and his real placement possibilities.

FUNDAMENTAL PRESUPPOSITIONS

A critical analysis of experiences at other centres has contributed to a definition of a few fundamental presuppositions.

Contemporaneous and Contextual Aspects of Training, Socialisation and Rehabilitation

Readaptation is a homogeneous and integrated process in which different specialist contributions need to be unified in an open environment. It attempts to enhance the capacities of the person who is handicapped and to overcome the social conditions that lead to his being socially isolated.

Inadequacy of Present Legislation

The rigid division into formative years, pre-established and out-of-date qualifications, the separation between education and training and outlet to a job and the closed and limited conception of the CPF hinder the development of programmes that are meaningful and appropriate to those who are handicapped.

The More Rigid the System of Qualifications, the Greater are the Placement Difficulties

Without neglecting professional/vocational competence it is necessary to provide flexible preparation and develop adaptability for a range of employment, bearing in mind that those who are handicapped very often find jobs in small firms and family businesses.

The Person who is Handicapped does not have sufficient Autonomy

Training and placement need to be studied in terms of the local area since those who are handicapped cannot seek work far from where they live. This requires very close relationship between the CPF, the firm and the neighbourhood.

The Widening of the Training Years

Training activities should be extended outside centres using all the opportunities that are offered by local employment and social activities in the neighbourhood.

The Training Cycle

This is articulated in three phases:

First Phase: Identifying individual needs, orientation and initial training. This phase can vary between 3 and 10 months according to the severity of the handicap. It includes the following elements:

a) Analysis and verification of the starting conditions
b) Diagnosis: rehabilitative needs of the individual elucidated by a multi-disciplinary team covering family, social, educational, medical and psychological aspects
c) Research: the recognition of the individual's habits, interests, potentials through stimulated conversations, training and expressive activities.

d) Recognition of Working Possibilities: through specialist examinations, analysis of the individual's home area and socialisation experiments.

e) Definition of the Readaptation Programme - by the assessment team.

f) Cultural Promotion and Initial General Training: 150 hours of scholastic recreational and group work, initial introduction to training in various fields (agriculture, industry, etc.), socialisation and the development of autonomy. The response of the individual determines entry to the next phase.

Second Phase: Qualification and apprenticeship. In this phase the specifically vocational problem is faced, and operations are carried out with the objective of attaining a qualification. It is articulated in:

a) Qualification

Formative and rehabilitative activities for the attainment of a vocational preparation which would permit entry into a firm.

b) Apprenticeships in firms

Apprenticeship for a completion of the preparation and a last element of socialisation in a non-protected environment.

c) Readaptation

Cultural and socialising activities.

Third Phase: Starting the job. The moment the client shows sufficient working capability he can be placed in a job, either inside the firm where he went through his apprenticeship or in another. This does not follow any pre-established timetable but the degree of maturity reached by the client. Placement may be individual, or in groups.

Immediately clients are placed in a job, there will be possibilities for others with handicaps in the area to enter the centre and a flow-through system will increase the extent to which all the needs of the district can be met. This will also depend on other operations in relation to living and economic aid which will facilitate the individual's re-entry into society and the local neighbourhood. These activities are carried out with the local authority services in the district.

Evaluation

The following tables give part of the information gained from a systematic enquiry into the work of the community. Where figures do not total 85, no response was available.

a) <u>The Sample</u>

1. Number of Cases

	Male	Female
under 18	3(3.5)	0
18-21	19(22.3)	4 4.7
22-25	13(15.3)	3 3.5
over 25	29(34.1)	14 16.5
	64(75.3)	21(24.7)

2. Diagnosis

	Number
1	6
2	29
3	11
4	8
5	2
6	24
7	5
	85

3. Previous Experience

Have always lived with the family				32
In an institution	under 1 yr.	1-3 yrs.	over 3	
	2	9	41	52
				84

4. Economic Conditions of Family

Very high	Good	Low	Very low	Total
2	51	21	4	78

5. Family's Attitude to Youth

Explicit Rejection	Valid Rejection	Low Degree of Acceptance	High Degree of Acceptance	Total
7	15	26	29	77

b) <u>Current Situation</u>

6. Where they live

With their families	Institutions	In other Non-Family Organisations	Total
51	4	30	85

7. Where they are integrated

Co-operative	On the Job Training	Hired	Other	Total
24	58	2	1	85

8. Type of Firm into which Integrated

Public Corporation	47
Co-operative	24
Private Craftsman's Shop	4
Private industry Metalwork	8
Other	2
	85

9. Number of Employees

Less than 30	30-100	100-300	More than 300	Total
16	22	17	30	85

10. Duration of Integration

Less than 6 months	6 months 1 year	1-2 years	More than 2 years	Total
14	19	14	38	85

11. Qualifications

No professional/vocational qualifications	37	85
With professional/voc/trade "	48	
Jobs corresponding to qualifications	14	48
Jobs not corresponding to qualifications	34	

The variety of jobs some of which require technical skills is very wide.

12. Working Situation

Alone	9	With other persons with handicaps	32
In small group	63	With persons without handicaps	52
In large group (over 6)	12		
	84		84
Work is varied	43	Work is simple	68
Repetitive	41	Work is complex	16
	84		84

c) <u>Follow-up Information</u>

13. Extent of Check-ups

Never 20*	Rarely 38	Monthly 10	Weekly 17	Total 85

* The 20 cases have become stable and require no further support.

14. Changes in Place of Work

None	Changed within same firm	Changed to another firm	Total
28	29	28	85

15. Socialisation

	Improvement					Total
	Process Reversed	Unchanged	Mild	Marked	Great	No answer	
Parents	2	13	23	23	24	0	85
Colleagues	0	10	22	30	21	2	85
Employers	1	13	26	27	17	1	85

16. Attitude to Work (Judged on Productivity I, Diligence II, Attainment of New Levels of Performance III)

	Colleagues	Employers
Improvement all three	37	35
Improvement on two	25	20
Improvement on one	14	14
Unchanged	6	9
Worse	2	2
No answer	1	5
	85	85

17. Opinion on Integration

	Favourable	Unfavourable	No answer	Total
Colleagues	81	4	0	85
Employers	77	7	1	85

CONCLUSION

The full report gives additional information about changes in opinion by colleagues/co-workers and employers and about behavioural changes. The overall result is to confirm that the scheme of training and introduction to work and personal autonomy is an interesting model for transitional arrangements.

V. DEVELOPING VOCATIONAL OPPORTUNITIES FOR HANDICAPPED PERSONS

by Prof. G. Thomas Bellamy
University of Oregon

This paper was prepared for the International Seminar on the Transition of Handicapped Adolescents from School to Employment or Further Study, in Auckland and Christchurch, New Zealand, September 1979.

The objective of this paper is to offer input and an American focus to international discussion of the question, "What are the means by which the handicapped person can participate in society with a life of dignity and purpose in the present employment climate?"

While the issues facing both handicapped individuals and those responsible for designing services for them are no doubt similar in most developed countries, any discussion of those issues necessarily reflects experiences and interests of the speaker. Important among these perspectives are: (a) reliance on services and programs in the United States to illustrate important service characteristics; (b) a particular concern with the vocational opportunities afforded severely handicapped persons; and (c) identification of service needs and practice-stretching models rather than simple description of current services and policies.

The paper first presents briefly the basis for including work opportunity as an element of an adult lifestyle with dignity and purpose and outlines the ideological, legal, and technological foundation for this view. Various issues that affect access to and retention in employment are then discussed to illustrate new or critical directions in vocational services.

IMPORTANCE OF VOCATIONAL OPPORTUNITIES

That work is a critical element in any adult lifestyle reflects several major trends in service delivery to handicapped individuals. This section outlines the impact of developing ideologies of normalization and integration, the expanding legal basis for equal work opportunity, and the availability of impersonal service technologies.

The concept of normalization as described by Nirje (1969) and Wolfensberger (1972) has become an increasingly pervasive referent in the evaluation of services for handicapped people. With its emphasis on access to normal opportunities and experiences, this concept has helped to shape both public and professional opinions. It is significant that major newspapers, including the Wall Street Journal (10 March, 1979) and the Guardian (13 June, 1979) have recently devoted space describing and advocating integrated community-based services for severely handicapped individuals. That such integration should include work opportunities is a clear implication of the normalization concept. Work is a normal and respected part of adult life in most developed countries and should be an option for all citizens. Total dependence on welfare or social service programs effectively prevents access to important aspects of a normal lifestyle.

Several recent legal developments in the United States have been congruent with this application of the normalization concept to the area of work. The implication of these and other legislative and judicial developments for vocational services and work opportunities is that procedures that discriminate against or segregate handicapped people can now be effectively challenged. The legal basis for full vocational participation is quickly developing.

Improvements in service technologies have also accentuated the importance of work opportunities for handicapped individuals. As techniques for vocational training, job supervision and job restructuring have developed, the presumption that many handicapped people were incapable of working has become less tenable. For example research on training and supervision techniques now has demonstrated that severely and profoundly retarded individuals can learn difficult vocational tasks and perform these at remunerative rates (e.g. Bellamy, Horner & Inman, 1979; Gold, 1974; Loos & Tizard, 1955).

The development of technologies for providing vocational services has reduced both the ideological and the legal basis on which job descrimination against handicapped individuals can be justified. Despite the fact that access to vocational opportunity is supported by widely accepted ideological positions, emerging legal developments, and an expanding array of service technologies, job options are nonetheless limited for most handicapped people. The remainder of this paper explores issues that appear to affect these options.

Issue 1: Access to Sheltered Work for Severely Handicapped Persons

Despite repeated demonstrations that severely handicapped persons can learn and perform a variety of work tasks, their access to sheltered workshops is limited. Instead, many of these individuals receive service only in day activity programs that attempt to provide treatment through academic instruction, preschool-like activities, and recreational events. They are excluded from vocational training and work opportunities on the presumption that vocational potential is lacking and they cannot gain entry to work programs because they do not have skills that could have resulted from such instruction. This segregation of severely handicapped adults into non-vocational programs and occupational centers is now in conflict with professional research that suggests that work is possible; professional and societal values that indicate work is desirable; and the changing economics of service.

Work is possible for severely handicapped adults

Research reported for more than two decades has repeatedly confirmed that severely handicapped individuals can acquire complex work-skills with systematic instruction. Previously incompetent individuals have learned such diverse skills as the assembly of bicycle pumps (Clarke & Hermelin, 1955); bicycle brakes (Gold, 1972); oscilloscope switches (Bellamy, Peterson, & Close, 1975); wiring harnesses (Hunter & Bellamy, 1977); nursery specimen cans (Karan, Eisner, & Endres, 1974); ballpoint pens (Martin & Flexer, 1975); chain saw blades (O'Neill & Bellamy, 1978); agricultural gleaning (Jacobs, 1976); and use of power equipment (Crosson, 1966).

Other research has identified supervision procedures which result in significant increases in work rates, often to levels above those associated with sheltered workshops [this literature has been surveyed by Bellamy (1976), and Martin & Pallotta-Cornick, (1979)]. Results of these research and program development activities contradict the prevalent view that severely handicapped individuals lack vocational potential or require extended periods of prevocational programming.

Segregation of severely handicapped individuals into activity and occupational centers can no longer be justified on the basis of individual capabilities.

Work is desirable for severely handicapped adults

Ideological and legal issues outlined earlier suggest that work is a critical component of a normal adult lifestyle in most developed countries. Given the documented potential of severely handicapped adults for vocational services, there appears little basis for providing vocational opportunities only to mildly handicapped persons. To segregate severely handicapped persons in activity programs effectively prevents access to important parts of normal lifestyle.

It is economically feasible to extend vocational opportunities

A final argument for the development of vocational opportunities for severely handicapped individuals relates to the cost of adult services. With the passage of PL 94-142, The Education of All Handicapped Children Act, severely handicapped people now enjoy public education programs through the age of 21. Unless new work options are developed, graduates from these extensive educational efforts will have no better future than the current total dependence on publicly supported residential and day activity programs. Provision of vocational training and work opportunities could reduce this lifelong dependency on income transfer, and contribute a part of both personal living and program expenses.

Until recently, economists have frequently argued against providing priority vocational services to severely retarded individuals because subsequent employment was less likely and less lucrative than if mildly handicapped individuals were served (Conley, 1972; Levitan & Taggart, 1977). However, this position may now be seriously questioned in light of the rapidly rising public cost of not providing vocational services and work opportunities. The current expense of housing, adult day programs, institutional care, and medical and social security benefits suggest that even partial employment that reduces public dependence could be cost-beneficial. Employment opportunities, even in sheltered employments, provide an attractive alternative to day activity programs that offer little promise of generating individual income to reduce reliance on public support.

A program model for including severely handicapped individuals in sheltered work settings has resulted from research at the University of Oregon. Fifteen severely and profoundly retarded individuals, most of whom had been extended residents of a large institution, began work in 1973 in a project designed to develop work-oriented alternatives to existing activity programs. These adults have learned to complete several jobs for regional industries including circuit board assembly, switch and instrument component assembly, hand soldering, complex sorting for materials reclamation, and construction of wiring harnesses, and assembly of mechanical components for chain saws, labeling devices, and irrigation equipment. With specialised supervision procedure, performance of several individuals has exceeded that expected of normal workers in the contracting industries (Bellamy, Peterson & Close, 1975; Bellamy, Inman & Yeates, 1978). Individual wages reflect this success. During the last 14 months workers in the program have averaged $1.40 per hour for all time spent in production. Although these earnings represent only half of the minimum wage in the United States, they are 2 1/2 times the national average for all retarded adults in sheltered workshops in the country.

In light of these considerations, it is recommended that the distinction between sheltered workshops and activity or occupational centers be replaced by a system that provides equal access to available work. Training and habilitation services based on individual needs could still be provided without policies and programs that unnecessarily restrict work opportunities for the more severely handicapped.

Issue 2: Availability of Work in Sheltered Workshops

Maintaining an adequate supply of appropriate work has been a persistent problem in sheltered workshops (Greenleigh Associates, 1975; U.S. Department of Labor, 1977). As a result, even those individuals who have gained entry to sheltered employment often miss the financial rewards of work. Low wages reflect sporadic access to real work options, insufficient design of available work so it fills available time, and lack of high production expectations. In a 1976 survey of sheltered workshops in the United States, Whitehead (1979) found average wages so low that "welfare" not "work" appears most descriptive of the programs. The average hourly wage in workshops was only $.58, or only one fifth of the national minimum wage.

The problem of low wages in workshops has been attributed to several factors, including reliance on overly simple and poorly priced work, lack of industrial engineering and work automation expertise, lack of skill training in workshops, and inadequate financing of work programs (Greenleigh Associates, 1975; Whitehead, 1979). National strategies to improve this situation have included development of training programs for workshop employees, providing competitive grants to workshops for business innovation and expansion, development of "set-aside" government contracts that give priority to workshops bidding on government work. Nevertheless, sheltered workshop wages are increasing less rapidly than the national minimum wage, and therefore, earnings in workshops appear increasingly to be tokens rather than wages.

One frequently-heard recommendation with relevance to this issue is that workshops with primary focus on extended employment be separated and organized differently from those emphasizing short-term training and open job placement. This specialization could allow greater investment in business-related equipment and personnel in the former case, and more emphasis on job training, open job placement, and follow-up in the latter. The "affirmative industry" model described by DuRand and DuRand (1978) provides one model for developing extended employment workshops. In this program emphasis is placed on management, operations, marketing and finance - traditional business concerns - rather than on the array of support services that are usually provided in sheltered workshops.

Issue 3: Skill Training for Available Jobs

The lack of training opportunities has been widely cited as a factor limiting access of handicapped individuals to both sheltered (Gold, 1974; Greenleigh Associates, 1975) and competitive work (Belmore and Brown, 1978; Sowers Thompson & Connis, 1979). Evidence cited earlier has established the potential of handicapped individuals to learn and perform jobs previously thought to be beyond their capabilities. Yet the training needed for competent performance of locally available work is often unavailable.

Instead of training, vocational service efforts have for some time focused on work experience and adjustment progress, personal counseling, and extended evaluation of current skills. In view of the available research on skill acquisition, it appears that these services may not be the most efficient means of promoting vocational competence. Bellamy, Horner & Inman (1979) suggested that current emphasis on support services like counseling and evaluation be replaced at least in part with an emphasis on direct intensive training and behaviour change programs. Staffing implications of such a change for sheltered workshops, school programs, and rehabilitation agencies are not insignificant. Considerable staff resources are now invested in professional counselors, social workers and evaluators who have periodic contact with handicapped clients. Effective training in many agencies will require reallocation of these resources to direct service staff members who have more continuous responsibility for client behavior, and who can implement training progress on an ongoing daily basis.

One example of the utility of intensive vocational training is the Food Service Vocational Training Program at the University of Washington (Sowers, Thompson & Connis, 1979). In this program, applied behavior analysis techniques are used to teach mildly and moderately retarded adults vocational skills required for beginning jobs in the food service industry. Trainees were referred from long-term sheltered workshop clients for whom traditional work experience, conseling and evaluation services had not resulted in consideration of open job placement. Training in the program includes development of skills in table laying, dishwashing, and utility maintenance as well as the support activities of remaining busy, managing personal time, and social instruction at work. When trainees learn these required skills they are moved to a second environment so that skills can be practiced under different supervision before open job placement. During the first two years of the program, seventeen program graduates were placed into a total of 31 jobs, with monthly wages ranging from $352-572, (Sowers, Thompson & Connis, 1979). Other model skill training programs are now developing in sheltered workshops (Bellamy, 1976; Karan, 1978; Wehman & Hill, 1979) and public school programs (Belmore and Brown, 1978).

The increasing success of these model training programs suggests that national policies and programs should be reevaluated to determine the optimum emphasis on traditional support services and direct training in the provision of vocational services. An additional commitment to training handicapped persons appears warranted.

Issue 4: Affirmative Action for Open Employment

A disproportionately large number of handicapped individuals are normally unemployed, and several positive discrimination measures have been proposed or tried to provide equal employment opportunity. Nevertheless, a persistent concern remains that handicapped individuals often are affected the most by adverse economic conditions (e.g., see Farber, 1968).

Affirmative action programs affecting handicapped individuals in the United States are mandated by the Rehabilitation Act of 1975 and the Vietnam Veterans Readjustment Act of 1974. Regulations extend to most employers who receive funds from or subcontract from federal agencies. Additional legislation is now under consideration in Congress to extend equal opportunity to handicapped people in all employment settings. Pati and Mezey (1978) describe a model affirmative action plan for an industry or business that complies with existing laws. Their plan includes:

a) Recruitment - Efforts must be made to attract qualified job applicants so that agencies and programs knowledgeable about handicapped persons are routinely contacted for referrals. Publicly posting notices of non-discriminatory personnel policies is a normal component of appropriate recruitment efforts.

b) _Selection_ - Several procedural guidelines apply to the collection and use of information in employee selection and hiring. The content of application forms, medical exams, and other evaluative devices now must be specifically tailored to the requests of individual jobs, rather than used in establishing general qualifications for employment.

c) _Accommodation_ - Affirmative action requires reasonable accommodation in the structure of duties and work environments to allow a handicapped employee to function effectively. Removal of architectural barriers, provision of special equipment for individuals with sensory impairments, and development of flexible working hours are examples of normally expected accommodations.

Whether an affirmative action strategy that relies on approved procedures for recruitment, selection, and accommodation will result in significant changes in employment opportunities is not yet clear. More stringent policies that mandated hiring quotas are clearly possible (and analogous to other civil rights enforcement activities in the United States); yet access to employment is a major interest to all segments of society, and the political impact of more stringent policies may be an effective deterrent to current implementation.

A second and more recent effort to expand employment opportunities for handicapped people in the United States is the 1979 revision of regulations for the Comprehensive Employment and Training Act of 1973. This program provides federally subsidized public service jobs to unemployed people whose families are economically disadvantaged. The current change in program administration allows any handicapped person to be served without regard to his or her family's economic status.

Therefore, while handicapped individuals have always been served in the program, their participation can now be expected to increase dramatically.

Issue 5: Increase and Maintenance of Productivity Levels

Low or erratic productivity often results in the termination of open employment and low, unreliable wages in sheltered workshops. Supervision procedures and support systems are needed that assist handicapped individuals increase productivity to acceptable levels and maintain those levels in extended employment periods.

Many programs and policies attribute productivity in trait-like fashion to individuals. That is, it is often assumed that individuals "possess" a given level of productivity and that appropriate program placement, wage levels, and job opportunities can be determined from that level. However, there are now considerable data to suggest that an individual's productivity may vary widely as a function of changes in supervision procedures, task requirements, living situations, and other factors (Bellamy, Horner & Inman, 1977; Edgerton & Bercovici, 1976). Such changes often affect job tenure and wages, and thus may represent significant barriers to employment.

To respond adequately to these barriers, policies and programs are needed that provide individually appropriate support in both sheltered and open employment. For example, workshops associated with our research at the University of Oregon define individualized supervision procedures for each worker. These procedures include specification of rules for supervisor contact with workers, special assistance requirements, payment schedules and scheduling of extra work breaks. The effect is to provide each individual with no more assistance than is necessary for independent work performance on each task, and to provide social, activity, and monetary rewards for sustained accurate work.

An example of the needed individualized support for handicapped people in open employment is a program in the State of Washington that assists handicapped individuals to work in food processing industries in eastern Washington. Operated jointly by the Teamster's Union and a local sheltered workshop, the program is one of several "Projects with Industry" grants funded by the National Rehabilitation Services Administration to promote cooperation between established business groups and sheltered work programs. During the last three years, this model program has placed more than 70 mildly handicapped individuals into union jobs in food processing plants. The program's unique feature is its provision of individualized independent living support to individuals outside the work situation, in order to minimize work disruption that could result from normal changes in living situations, friendships, recreational opportunities, and daily problems associated with personal care, residence maintenance and community living.

These and other model programs suggest that the productivity of handicapped people can remain high if adequate individualized support is available. As employment policies are evaluated it would appear more useful to focus on the variety of support services that may be required to maintain high productivity rather than on the definition of productivity levels assumed to be characteristic of individuals with various handicaps.

Issue 6: Disincentives to Work

Many handicapped individuals in the United States enjoy a variety of government benefits, including income support and medical services from federal agencies, residential and activity programs supported by state agencies, and a variety of local social service benefits. Clearly, these benefits are critical for stable community life, but their administration often provides disincentives for handicapped individuals to accept employment.

Disincentives arise through the reduction or loss of benefits as the handicapped individual becomes more productive and, therefore, able to meet his or her own needs. It would seem possible to coordinate reduction in benefits with increases in individual earnings so that work is encouraged. However, two problems have persisted in the United States. First, significant month-to-month variation in earnings is not uncommon for many handicapped individuals. This may result from inconsistent availability of work in sheltered employment (Whitehead, 1979) or the short duration of many competitive jobs (e.g., see Edgerton and Bercovici, 1976). Since high wages for only a few months often remove an individual's eligibility for benefits, there may be considerable risk associated with improvements in productivity.

A second disincentive reflects the cost of replacing individual benefits. It is now possible to lose publicly supported medical and social service benefits, when employment is secured, although earnings may not be sufficient to replace the support which was lost.

To remove these barriers to employment, public benefits and job opportunities should be coordinated so that individuals can take advantage of short-term work opportunities without jeopardizing long-term benefits; receive special support as required to maintain employment; and gradually accept the cost of medical social services as income increases.

Issue 7: Development of Intermediate Work Opportunities

Many handicapped individuals are capable of performing work required in open employment, but access to or maintenance of employment is limited by factors other than job demands. Such factors include, for example, the expense of retraining when tasks change, requirements for additional supervision, or ongoing assistance in adapting to social requirements of the work place. Intermediate work opportunities, between current sheltered and competitive placement, are needed.

Basic to this notion of intermediate work opportunities is the belief that many moderately and severely handicapped persons are capable of high productivity levels in carefully structured employment situations. Therefore, efforts to improve job opportunities should focus not only on the quality of rehabilitation effort, but also on the structure of employment opportunities themselves. Options can be developed to combine structured individual training and supervision with adequate work in industry-like settings that emphasize business rather than service issues. As such, an intermediate employment option could be a sheltered workshop that was organized for highly productive, extended employment; an enclave within industry; a community-based, worker-owned cooperative; or some other arrangement. In any case, policies supporting intermediate employment will have to provide adequate incentives for employers and a provision for ongoing or recurrent personal support for handicapped workers.

SUMMARY

The issues raised in this paper follow from the presumption that _all_ handicapped individuals have the potential for and the right for equal employment opportunity. There are now several model programs that illustrate effective methods of extending work to more severely handicapped people, improving training and support services, and increasing employment tenure. Policies are needed that support these efforts and extend them to daily community services.

REFERENCES

Bellamy, G. T. "Habilitation of the severely and profoundly retarded: A review of research on work productivity", in T. Bellamy (Ed.), _Habilitation of severely and profoundly retarded adults_, Vol. I. Eugene, Oregon: University of Oregon Center on Human Development, 1976.

Bellamy, G. T., Horner, R. H. & Inman, D. P. (Eds.), _Habilitation of severely and profoundly retarded adults_, Vol. II. Eugene, Oregon: University of Oregon Center on Human Development, 1977.

Bellamy, G. T., Horner, R. H. & Inman, D. P. *Vocational habilitation of severely retarded adults: A direct service technology*. Baltimore: University Park Press, 1979.

Bellamy, G. T., Inman, D. P. & Yeates, J, "Evaluation of a procedure for production management with the severely retarded", *Mental Retardation*, 1978 16 (4), 317-319.

Bellamy, G., Peterson, L., & Close, D. "Habilitation of the severely and profoundly retarded: Illustrations of competence", *Educating the Mentally Retarded*, 1975, 10, 174-186.

Belmore, K. J. & Brown, L. "A job skill inventory strategy designed for severely handicapped potential workers", in N. Haring and D. Bricker (Eds.), *Teaching the severely handicapped*, Vol. III. Columbus, Ohio: Special Press, 1978.

Clarke, A., & Hermelin, F. "Adult imbeciles: Their abilities and trainability", *The Lancet*, 1955, 2, 337-339.

Conley, R. *The economics of mental retardation*. Baltimore: Johns Hopkins Press, 1972.

Crosson, J. *The experimental analysis of vocational behavior in severely retarded males*. Doctoral dissertation. University of Oregon, 1966.

DuRand, L. & DuRand, J. *The Affirmative Industry*. St. Paul, Minnesota: Minnesota Diversified Industries, 1978.

Edgerton, R. & Bercovici, S. "The cloak of competence: Years later", *American Journal of Mental Deficiency*, 1976, 80, 485-497.

Farber, B. *Mental Retardation: Its Social Context and Social Consequences*. Boston: Houghton Mifflin Company, 1968.

Gold, M. "Stimulus factors in skill training of the retarded on a complex assembly task: Acquisition, transfer and retention", *American Journal of Mental Deficiency*, 1972, 76, 517-526.

Gold, M. "Redundant cue removal in skill training for the retarded", *Education and Training of the Mentally Retarded*, 1974, 9(1), 5-8.

Greenleigh Associates. *The role of the sheltered workshop in the rehabilitation of the severely handicapped.* Report to the Department of Health, Education and Welfare, Rehabilitation Services Administration, New York, 1975.

Halderman vs. Pennhurst, (Eastern District, Pennsylvania), 1977.

Hunter, J., & Bellamy, G. T. "Cable harness construction for severely retarded adults: A demonstration of training technique", *AAESPH Review*, 1977, 1(7), 2-13.

Jacobs, J. W. "Retarded persons as gleaners", *Mental Retardation*, 1976, 14(6), 42-43.

Karan, O. C. *Habilitation practices with the severely developmentally disabled*, Vol. II. Madison, Wisconsin University: Wisconsin University Research and Training Center in Mental Retardation, 1978.

Karan, R., Eisner, M., & Endres, R. "Behavior modification in a sheltered workshop for severely retarded students", *American Journal of Mental Deficiency*, 1974, 79, 338-347.

Laski, Frank J. "Legal strategies to secure entitlement to services for severely handicapped persons", in G. T. Bellamy, G. O'Connor and O. Karan (Eds.), *Vocational rehabilitation of severely handicapped persons: Contemporary service strategies.* Baltimore: University Park Press, 1979.

Levitan, S., & Taggart, R. *Jobs for the disabled.* Baltimore: Johns Hopkins University Press, 1977.

Loos, F. & Tizard, J. "The employment of adult imbeciles in a hospital workshop", *American Journal of Mental Deficiency*, 1955, 59, 395-403.

Martin, A.S. & Flexer, R.W. *Three studies on training work skills and work adjustment with the severely retarded.* Monograph No. 5. Lubbock, Texas: Texas Tech University, Research and Training Center in Mental Retardation, 1975.

Martin, G., & Pallotta-Cornick, A. "Behavior modification in sheltered workshops and community group homes for the retarded: Current status and future considerations", in G. Hammerlynch (Ed.), *Applied behavior analysis techniques for the developmentally disabled.* New York: Brunner-Mazel, 1979.

Nirje, B. "The normalization principle and its human management implications", in R. Kugel and W. Wolfensberger (Eds.), *Changing Patterns of Residential Services for the Mentally Retarded*. Washington, D.C.: President's Committee on Mental Retardation, 1969, 179-195.

O'Neill, C., & Bellamy, G. T. "Evaluation of a procedure for teaching saw chain assembly to a severely retarded woman", *Mental Retardation*, 1978, 16(1) 37-41.

Pati, G. C., and Mezey, M. J., "Designing an affirmative action program for the handicapped", *Training and Development Journal*, June, 1978, 14-22.

Sowers, J., Thompson, L., & Connis, R., "The food service vocational training program", in T. Bellamy, G. O'Connor and O. Karan (Eds.), *Vocational rehabilitation of severely handicapped persons: Contemporary service strategies*. Baltimore: University Park Press, 1979.

U.S. Department of Labor, *Sheltered workshop study, Worksurvey*, Vol. I. Washington, D.C.: U.S. Department of Labor, 1977.

Wehman, P., & Hill, J. *Vocational training and placement of severely disabled persons: Project employability*, Volume I. Richmond, Virginia: Virginia Commonwealth University, 1979.

Whitehead, C. W., "Sheltered workshops in the decade ahead: Work and wages or welfare", in G. T. Bellamy, G. O'Connor and O. Karan (Eds.), *Vocational rehabilitation of severely handicapped persons: Contemporary service strategies*. Baltimore: University Park Press, 1979.

Wolfensberger, W., (Ed.). *The principle of normalization in human services*. Downsview, Toronto, Canada: National Institute on Mental Retardation, York University Campus, 1972.

VI. EMPLOYING THE HANDICAPPED IN SWEDISH INDUSTRY

By Anne Marie Quarfort and Göte Bernhardsen,
Swedish Government Commission on Long-term Employment

[Editorial note: This chapter is an abridgement of a paper contributed to the Handicapped Adolescent programme in 1980 describing a project on how to re-employ occupationally handicapped people in a company. It is of particular interest because it illustrates the importance of action in the work place. Two background comments are necessary. The first is to note the changing concept of handicap as individuals move from education and training to employment. Occupational handicap in this paper includes social problems. Secondly the concept of "Adjustment teams" is a Swedish development of considerable interest. These are groups formed in work places with representatives of management, unions and the Labour Board whose tasks are to study the working environment and facilitate the employment of the occupationally handicapped.]

RE-EMPLOYMENT IN THE PRIVATE SECTOR

Objective and Plan of the Project

The project aimed at evaluating the following:
i) Current measures of labour market and personnel policy tried out within the project to facilitate the re-employment of occupationally handicapped persons.
ii) Measures of labour market and personnel policy suggested by the Swedish Commission on Long-Term Employment Policy and the Volvo Company to facilitate the re-employment of occupationally handicapped persons.
iii) The comprehensive picture of these measures of labour market and personnel policy.

Evaluation has been mainly intended to illustrate the way in which companies can provide persons in danger of being eliminated with continued productive occupation, with the aid of measures of both labour market and personnel policy. It was further intended to provide ways of re-employing occupationally handicapped persons in companies with the aid of such measures. Extremely important basic material was provided by a fact-finding enquiry carried out with the occupationally handicapped people themselves. The empirical part of the project was carried out at two Volvo units: the assembly section of the Volvo Torslanda Plant in Gothenburg and the engine factory of the Volvo Skövde Plants. It was developed in four stages:

>Stage 1.
>a) fact-finding concerning the occupationally handicapped at the two units, and work place analysis;
>b) fact-finding concerning the measures of labour market and personnel policy applied at the units before the project started.
>
>Stage 2.
>Experimental activities and reinforcement of the present measures.
>
>Stage 3.
>Evaluation of experimental activities.
>
>Stage 4.
>The drawing of conclusions.

The project was jointly conducted by the Government Commission on Long-Term Employment Policy and AB Volvo. The Institute for Industrial Evolution AB (INDEVO) - a development and consultant company - took part in the practical work, was responsible for evaluation of the project and wrote the report.

Fact-finding about occupationally handicapped people within the companies

At the Volvo Skövde Plants the Company Health Care Services carried out a comprehensive survey concerning, for example, the occurrence of occupationally handicapped employees, the causes and degrees of severity of their problems, the level of health and comfort experience, job adaptation and the occurrence of short-term and long-term illnesses.

The results indicated that about 25 per cent of the plant employees and about 21.5 per cent of the staff employees consisted of occupationally handicapped people. This corresponded to 24.5 per cent of all the employees. The percentage of severe cases was not quite 7 per cent among the plant employees and not quite 4 per cent among the staff employees.

Of the occupationally handicapped who worked at the plant about two-thirds suffer mainly from physical problems. Lumbar complaints and cardiac and vascular illnesses were most usual. Mental retardation made up the main problem for about 25-30 per cent while social problems - primarily alcoholism - made up 6 per cent of the main problems encountered by the occupationally handicapped. Among the staff employees the social problems occurred to a smaller extent, while otherwise the pattern was about the same.

On the whole, the physical problems increased very rapidly with increasing age, while the mental problems increased much more slowly; the social problems occurred to roughly the same extent among younger and older people. Mental and social problems were over-represented among the younger people and physical problems among the older people.

The percentage of occupationally handicapped persons among the plant employees was higher among women than among men in the same age groups. This also applied among staff employees with the exception of the age group 40-49 years. Occupationally handicapped persons with physical problems appreciated their health and contentment on average to a greater extent than handicapped people with other problems, particularly those with social problems. The level of contentment was poorest in the lowest age groups and best in the highest age groups.

The staff employees interviewed who were occupationally handicapped had stated that their health and contentment on the whole were better than those of the occupationally handicapped among the plant employees.

According to the appraisal of the supervisors and foremen, about 5 per cent of the occupationally handicapped could not carry out their job in an acceptable way. This applied to a considerably greater extent among the younger than among the older (10 per cent between 20 and 29 years old and 2-3 per cent of the over-50s. <u>It was primarily younger people with alcohol problems and other social problems who could not carry out their work in an acceptable way</u>.

The appraisal of the Company Health Care Services with respect to job adaptation from the viewpoint of health among occupationally handicapped showed that adaptation was better on the whole among staff employees than among plant employees. Furthermore, it was better among the older than among the younger, and better among men than among women.

A follow-up was carried out on people with a high rate of absenteeism (absent more than 10 times during the last year). The result showed that among the occupationally handicapped, the proportion with a high level of absenteeism was more than twice as high as among other plant employees. The differences were considerably greater in the lowest age groups.

In connection with a study of long-term illnesses, it was found that periods of sickness of more than 42 days were more than six times as frequent among occupationally handicapped as among other plant employees.

At the Company Health Care Services in the Skövde Plants, the following conclusions were drawn from the follow-up:

> "Both the frequency and the number of days off can be influenced through measures that are adopted or initiated at the work place. In order to make such initiatives possible, it is important to organise, not only follow-up of the state of health of occupationally handicapped as well as their working situation and job adaptation, but also follow-up of and recurrent contacts with those suffering from long-term illnesses. These follow-ups and contacts should be co-ordinated by the Company Health Care Services but require greater personal resources than those at the disposal of the Company Health Care Services today."

At the <u>Torslanda Plant</u>, at the beginning of the project, very little had been done concerning fact-finding and the rectification of problems for the occupationally handicapped. Because of this, it was decided that no comprehensive survey was to be carried out with respect to them. Instead, a number of target groups were identified within which it was assumed that the frequency of occupationally handicapped was high. These target groups included people with long-term absenteeism, people with a high level of short-term absenteeism, occupationally handicapped persons, and those who had been working in semi-sheltered activities.

A selection was then made from these target groups and personal interviews involving a total of 63 people were carried out by a Company nurse. These indicated that 48 people were occupationally handicapped. The main causes of the problems encountered by 80 per cent of these people were of a physical and mental nature (medical obstacles); for 16 per cent (seven people) the origin lay in the way in which the individual experienced the job situation. The remaining cases suffered from various social problems which appeared to be of considerably more importance in the case of supplementary interviews carried out by a welfare officer.

The results from the Torslanda Plant indicated that at least 15 per cent of the employees were occupationally handicapped. However, the reliability of this calculation was low. Overall the result indicates that the average for both units consisted of a proportion of occupationally handicapped of at least 20, probably 20-25 per cent.

To obtain factual information about the occupationally handicapped, interview surveys were conducted among the employees in semi-sheltered work in the Torslanda Plant and the Skövde Plant. The results of this are described in a report from INDEVO to the Commission.

Fact-finding about the occupationally handicapped outside the regular labour market

One of the objectives of the project was to evaluate the conditions for finding placements for these people. One important requirement, therefore, was a study of the conditions whereby the people in the vocational rehabilitation centre can accept a job in the regular labour market. To clarify this matter, an inventory was made of the Vocational Rehabilitation Centres in Gothenburg and Skövde. The following are some of the results that emerged from this:

- The most usual handicaps among those in the Vocational Rehabilitation Centres consisted of mental and social/medical problems.
- The mental problems were over-represented among the women and the social/medical problems among the men.
- For about 20 per cent of the people in the vocational rehabilitation queue, the cause of the problem was stated to be associated with earlier work.
- About half the people in the vocational rehabilitation queue were found to have a work capacity of more than two-thirds in relation to a performance considered normal.
- Among those applying for vocational rehabilitation it was estimated that about 12 per cent could accept a job that did not make any special demands on the individual. About half of them could accept work, being able to meet the special demands made by the job.
- A comparison between the fact-finding with respect to occupationally handicapped people within Volvo and those in the vocational rehabilitation queue showed that the social/medical problems were three to four times more frequent among the latter and that their work capacity on average was lower than among the occupationally handicapped within the companies.

Work place analysis

An extremely important prerequisite of all adjustment work was systematized knowledge concerning the demands made by a job. For this reason, at the Torslanda Plant work-place analysis was initiated during the course of the project. In the Skövde Plants, work-place analysis had been carried out for a long time.

Analysis in the Torslanda Plant was done by a special inventory group consisting of a trade union representative, a production technician, an industrial safety engineer and a company doctor. It was carried out at 1,370 work places, corresponding to 2,163 jobs. The following are some of the facts that emerged:

65 per cent of the jobs made great demands on arms and legs

59 per cent of the jobs made great demands on the back

53 per cent of the jobs were carried out standing up

50 per cent of the jobs consisted of constrained movements

49 per cent of the jobs made great demands on legs and feet

29 per cent of the jobs were carried out both sitting and standing

27 per cent of the jobs required great physical endurance

13 per cent of the jobs implied work carried out above shoulder height

9 per cent of the jobs made great demands on the eyes

5 per cent of the jobs were isolated

5 per cent of the jobs were carried out sitting down.

Experimental activities

As a background and a basis for comparison for the experimental activities, investigations were made into how the work of solving the problems of occupationally handicapped could be carried out before a project was initiated.

Most of the money made available through labour market policy measures had previously been spent on grants towards semi-sheltered work places at Volvo. So far as the occupationally handicapped were concerned, this represented about US$160,000 at the Skövde Plants and US$210,000 at the Torslanda Plant during 1975.

The personnel policy measures executed on behalf of the occupationally handicapped during 1975 at the Skövde Plants amounted to 20-30 man/years and at the Torslanda Plant to 16-29 man/years. Expressed in money, this corresponds to US$240,000-480,000 at each Volvo unit.

The tests carried out within the project were structured into three main groups:

- technical measures
- organisational measures
- attitude-influencing measures

The project plan included a number of technical measures to try to solve the difficulties experienced by the occupationally handicapped with physical problems. Nine of these were implemented at the Skövde Plants and two in the Torslanda Plant.

The evaluation of the technical measures introduced at both the Skövde Plants and the Torslanda Plant showed that all were financially profitable. This applied to the Company, the Government and the community as a whole. Table 1 summarises a few of the financial results of the measures studied.

Table 1

SUMMARY OF PROFITABILITY FROM THE IMPLEMENTATION OF TECHNICAL MEASURES

(Recalculated to present values, US dollars)

	Skövde Plants				Torslanda Plant
	1	2	3	4	1
Financial result, community	50,700	40,000	51,800	28,900	11,600
Financial result, company	2,900	1,100	2,600	2,700	2,000
Financial result, Government	23,900	18,200	26,600	5,700	4,800

Within the project, the work of the adjustment teams at both the Volvo units was re-organised and considerably intensified. The extensive work carried out by the various adjustment teams during the project showed that important results can be attained through their activity. Some calculated examples based on results attained in practice also showed that the work can be financially profitable. Experience of experiments with working groups (for example three people carrying out two jobs), assistants and supervisors indicated that more work should be based on solutions of this type.

One of the main objectives of the project was to show that it should be possible with the aid of measures both of labour market policy and personnel policy to provide employment for unemployed occupationally handicapped persons in the regular labour market. The conditions for attempting to carry out <u>integration</u> were changed to a considerable extent, however, during the introductory phase of the project, due to the extensive cuts in production at Volvo, which stopped recruitment for a long period. The production changes also implied a deterioration in the internal situation involving the location of occupationally handicapped people who were already employed. This meant that integration possibilities worsened in two respects.

Attempts at integration at the Torslanda Plant were started in March 1977. By October the same year, no one had yet been integrated there. The experiments showed how important active mediation activities between individuals and work places are, where a vital condition is detailed knowledge about the conditions of the individual and the demands made by the job, and that the availability of suitable jobs is essential if integration is to be successful.

A wide range of <u>informational activity</u> was carried out within the limits of the project, particularly at the Torslanda Plant. This was done in the light of the general attitude towards and the level of knowledge about the situation of the occupationally handicapped being decisive in the solution of their employment problems.

By way of summary it can be said that the attitude-influencing measures directly initiated by the project had a positive effect on the possibilities of solving the situation of the occupationally handicapped. Training and informational activities at different levels are a vital condition for success.

Conclusions

- The semi-sheltered activities had great positive significance for the occupationally handicapped.

- The adjustment teams were very important and their work was shown to produce effects which easily exceed the resources invested.

- Technical measures can provide positive results for the individuals and financial profitability for both the Company and the community.

- Training and informational activities at different levels made up a vital condition if the problems experienced are to be solved.

- Company Health Care Services played a central part in adjustment work during the project; it was, however, important to solve as many problems as possible in the main organisational stream.

- It was important to follow up job adjustment at regular intervals among all the employees, particularly those with a high rate of short-term or long-term absenteeism, to develop work places according to individual capabilities, and to exercise relocation when necessary.

- The existing measures of labour market policy had been mostly used for the adaptation of people suffering from physical problems. The fact-finding indicated that about two-thirds suffered primarily from physical troubles and one-third from mental and social problems. However, all the facts indicated that from the viewpoint of both Company and community finances, the mental and social problems involved greater cost than the physical problems. It was also noted that it was primarily young people who suffered from mental and social problems. Development of new labour market policies should take these factors into consideration.

- Many of the measures that were planned and implemented during the course of the project consisted of "spot" activities and were of a relatively short-term nature. It is important for adaptation work, however, that measures for occupationally handicapped persons should be integrated in long-term planning as well - for example in connection with production processing or construction work. In fact this was done for one of the units studied.

- The resources allocated by the labour market authorities to mediation work appear to have been insufficient. There must be active contact between planners and the work place (where a great deal is known about the conditions of the individual and the demands made by the job) if the integration of retarded people is to be successful.

- The conclusion was that if you can use efficient measures of labour market and personnel policy to decrease the proportion of employees who cannot carry out their job in an acceptable way, then there is a very large range of investment for this work.

EFFORTS TO INCREASE THE EMPLOYMENT OF OCCUPATIONALLY HANDICAPPED PERSONS IN THE PUBLIC SECTOR

During the autumn of 1976 the Government Commission on Long-Term Employment Policy launched a two-year experimental scheme at six national departments and within two local government administrations with the aim of activating the work of adjustment teams in these sectors. The initial period of experimentation, which ended in the autumn of 1977, was devoted to the establishment of adjustment teams within the organisations concerned and, subsequently, to placement activities for unemployed occupationally handicapped persons with a well-defined order of priorities. The second period, from the autumn of 1977 until mid-1978 was more specifically concerned with internal adjustment questions within the organisations and with following up the recruitment of occupationally handicapped persons that began during the initial phase. The following is a summary of a report prepared for the Commission by Carl Magnus Tunevall.

The size of the organisations involved and the nature of their activities varied considerably. Personnel strength ranged from about 200 to about 7,000. Salaried occupations predominated within some; the local government administrations incorporated a very wide range of posts; one of the organisations involved consisted mainly of a large printing business. This variation was deliberate, one of the purposes of the experiment being to furnish the broadest possible experience of the opportunities and impediments associated with the employment of occupationally handicapped persons in different conditions.

The experiment was built up round the adjustment groups in the organisations concerned. Within many of the organisations, however, these teams had only existed in a formal context prior to the experiment. Insofar as they had pursued any activities worth mentioning, these had mainly been concerned with personnel transfers and other internal matters.

Purpose and Methodology - First Phase

The scheme was designed to include a number of measures aimed at improving the initial prospects of the placement activities which the experiment was intended to bring about, namely:

i) Reinforced representation of the various parties in the adjustment groups which, among other things, meant that the local employment offices were expected to devote far greater resources to their participation in the teams of the organisations involved.

ii) Intensified information for various key persons within the organisation concerned about instruments of labour market policy, problems of occupational handicap and so forth. Written information to all employees concerning the experiment and the activities of the adjustment groups.
iii) The charting of a wide selection of appointments within the organisations concerned, to provide documentation for the identification of suitable jobs for occupationally handicapped persons.

While these preparations were in progress, the local employment offices in the three main experimental areas were instructed to select job applicants with registered occupational handicaps. The aim in making this selection was to achieve a structure that would provide the closest possible reflection, in terms of occupational handicap, age, sex, etc., of the larger population of occupationally handicapped persons the various offices had to deal with. The sample could not be made completely random, however, because participation in the experiment had to be made subject to certain criteria: for example, job applicants could not be involved by other measures which would be disrupted by participation in the experiment, they had to be sufficiently rehabilitated for job placement, they had to be interested in one of the activities covered by the experiment, and so on. This meant that certain difficult cases had to be excluded, but their exclusion was partly offset by the exclusion of particularly straightforward cases as well.

Altogether more than 200 people of different ages were selected for introduction to the organisations taking part in the experimental scheme. As a form of preparation they were interviewed in accordance with a questionnaire corresponding directly to the instrument used in the charting of appointments within the authorities concerned. This parallel structure has also made it possible to make direct comparisons between job descriptions and the demands and limitations with regard to working life the applicants were asked to describe in their interviews. The personnel administering the interviews included industrial psychologists.

About one-fourth of the group had orthopaedic handicaps and another fourth mental handicaps. But there were also people with other sorts of handicap such as social-medical, intellectual, cardio-vascular and pulmonary diseases and vision defects.

Placement results

Roughly one-third of the more than 200 people in the sample population obtained some form of employment or vocational practice - usually employment on normal terms - following their introduction to the authorities taking part in the experimental scheme. Two-thirds of them got a semi-sheltered job.

An equally considerable number obtained employment or vocational practice during the six-month placement period with firms not taking part in the experimental scheme. Many of these placements were a direct result of the Employment Service devoting special resources to all the members of the experimental population.

In this way more than half the members of the experimental population were found some kind of employment or vocational practice during the term of the experiment. Of the remainder, one group was "written off" for the purposes of the experiment after declining offers of employment at one of the authorities taking part in the experiment; another group was judged to be more in need of other measures such as education, training or work testing than job placement; and a third group was still being dealt with by one of the adjustment groups when the first period of the experiment ended in the autumn of 1977.

These results are very good compared with the results presented in the statistics of employment offices concerning measures on behalf of job applicants with occupational handicaps. In recent years the proportion placed in the regular market has been in the region of 10-12 per cent per annum. At the same time it should be pointed out that these comparisons should not be pushed too far. For one thing, the representativeness of the experimental population was not proven, although initiated assessments by the employment offices indicate that the samples were a good reflection of the clients the Employment Service normally has to deal with. Secondly the resources devoted to adjustment activities were far above the normal level and implied special efforts by the various parties represented in the adjustment groups. The positive image of the results of the experiment is reinforced, however, when one studies individual people who obtained work through the experiment after, in many cases, a highly varied occupational background with repeated short-time engagements.

The Second Phase

More than 85 per cent of those who had found employment during the first experimental period still held the same job during the follow-up phase in the summer of 1978. More than a third had regular employment and others semi-sheltered employment. Table 2 shows what had happened to the job applicants included in the experimental group.

All of those with hearing impairment and with intellectual handicaps obtained employment. But for people

Table 2

WHAT HAPPENED TO THE JOB APPLICANTS, 1978-79

208 Job Applicants were formed into an Experimental Group, Spring 1977	
7 of the applicants were excluded from the experiment because, upon closer examination, they were not deemed to be occupationally handicapped.	27 were excluded from the course before being presented to any of the participating authorities' adjustment groups.

174 persons were discussed in the Adjustment Groups	
FOR 80 THIS LED TO EMPLOYMENT OF SOME FORM WITHIN THE PARTICIPATING AUTHORITIES

In three cases, this was a matter of temporary employment, acting employment and relief work which ceased during the period and which was not renewed for various reasons at the end of the experiment. | 94 WERE EXCLUDED FROM THE TRIAL AFTER CONSIDERATION BY ADJUSTMENT GROUP

Common reasons for exclusions were refusal to accept offered work, a shortage of suitable working duties or that other measures were deemed more appropriate. |

POSITION UPON FOLLOW-UP JUNE/JULY 1978	
69 FROM THE EXPERIMENTAL GROUP WERE STILL EMPLOYED BY THE PARTICIPATING AUTHORITIES

Of these,

24 had a normal position;

42 had semi-sheltered employment;

3 had practice of relief work, with a decision for semi-sheltered employment.

8 WITH PERMANENT EMPLOYMENT HAVE LEFT THE EXPERIMENTAL AUTHORITIES:

One case with a proposal for semi-sheltered employment was not decided until after the experimental period. | IN FOLLOWING UP ALL "EXCLUDED" IT EMERGED THAT

26 were at work in the open labour market;

35 had some form of sheltered or semi-sheltered employment;

12 were undergoing training or some other measure;

16 were still looking for work;

24 were on the sick list or receiving sickness benefit or a premature pension.

One case was taken up afresh by an adjustment group. |

with vision defects the result was not so good - only about 67 per cent succeeding. The social/medical handicapped was a group that found it most difficult to obtain a job, even with special arrangements.

During the second experimental phase, work was concentrated on internal adjustment questions, such as replacements, information and working environment work. New jobs were also found during this period. Among others, five occupationally handicapped with a long period of education obtained higher administrative posts with an authority.

The information and training efforts applied during the initial experimental stage were followed up only to a limited extent. The adjustment groups had difficulty in initiating measures to provide better work possibilities for the occupationally handicapped at the work place.

Difficulties in the way of placing the occupationally handicapped

The difficulties encountered in the course of our experimental activities in the public sector may be summarised as follows:

- obtaining dependable information about the job applicants;
- finding suitable new jobs while vacancies have often to be filled by permanent staff. Furthermore, not all jobs are open to external recruitment owing to regulations requiring a certain amount of internal training and experience;
- establishing functional channels for the internal follow-up of new employees and bringing about co-operation with, among others, the social welfare authorities in individual cases;
- coping with follow-up and supporting measures for social/medically and mentally/occupationally handicapped with problems outside the work place;
- spreading the practical responsibility for the rehabilitation work;
- shortage of personnel capable of dealing with rehabilitation work;
- reaching the employees with information about the work of the adjustment group. The management groups were particularly difficult to reach with information and attitude influence;
- establishing priorities between various urgent groups;
- problems with social/medical and mentally handicapped individuals were the most difficult to solve.

These problems, however, do not occur solely in the public sector; they are equally common in the private firms.

Economic Gains to Society

A simple arithmetical example can be used to demonstrate that the economic gain to society from employment of occupationally handicapped individuals is substantial. This is true even when relatively generous grants for semi-sheltered employment are paid. A comparison can be made between semi-sheltered employment and unemployment which is the most common alternative. Calculations show that the social gain when semi-sheltered employment is available can be roughly estimated at US$5,700 per annum per employee during the four-year period for which the grant is usually payable.

If we count only that proportion of the occupationally handicapped who, without the experiment, would probably have been either unemployed or on the sick list - more than half - the profit to society can be roughly estimated at barely US$800,000 during a four-year period. This applies even in comparison with the alternative that is most expensive to society - semi-sheltered employment. The calculated profit would be so much the greater if allowance were made for the whole of the group employed through the experiment and of the fact that a substantial number of individuals obtained employment without, or with smaller, grants than are payable for semi-sheltered employment.

Less Need of Care

Apart from the immediate economic effects, substantial savings may also be counted upon in the form of less need of care and less load on the social machinery. The economic gains are also substantial for the individual - other positive factors being all the values that cannot be calculated in financial terms - such as social contacts, meaningfulness and identification in daily life, and so on.

What proved most difficult was to make an exact calculation of the economic effects for the experimental authorities. It was remarkable, however, that the frequently biggest "additional costs" were due to the need for follow-up measures, additional administrative work, etc. The pure production effects of the capacity of the occupationally handicapped to work, which in certain cases was limited, was largely covered by the grants for semi-sheltered employment.

VII. THE ROLES AND NEEDS OF PARENTS OF HANDICAPPED ADOLESCENTS

By Peter Mittler, Sally Cheseldine and Helen McConachie,
Hester Adrian Research Centre, University of Manchester

Three main phases can be detected in the relationship between professionals and the parents of handicapped children. For many years parents received little or no help from professionals and were largely unsupported. Such advice as they received tended to be negative and rarely included practical suggestions on what they could do to help their child at home. Indeed, parents were at one time frequently advised to place the child in residential care. The second phase, beginning towards the end of the 1960s, took the form of training parents to use some of the techniques previously restricted to professionals and regarding them as 'co-therapists'. Many parents were quick to learn these techniques and put them to good use with their children; research workers began to investigate the most effective methods of training parents and enlisting their help in carrying out programmes devised by professionals (O'Dell, 1974; Cunningham, 1975).

But although parents and children may have benefited from such programmes, professionals have largely worked on the assumption that they know best what the child should learn and therefore what the parents should do at home. It is not surprising that some parents have felt that such a one-way approach did not meet their needs and resented the implicit assumption that professionals knew what was best for their child. Furthermore, parents have not always been able to meet the demands of the programmes being devised by professionals; it has been suggested that "some professionals have been so busy teaching parents to be teachers that there may not be enough time left for parents to be parents" (Mittler, 1979). Such a 'transplant' model is likely to be rejected (Jeffree, 1980).

We are now entering a third phase in which attempts are being made to develop a partnership on a basis of equality. Both sides contribute their own areas of knowledge and skill but parents are encouraged to retain their sense of identity as parents and to remain true to their own natural style of relating to their child. The approach starts with the needs of the child in a family context and tries to mobilise the existing resources of the family. Individual members of the family may acquire specific skills and techniques as a means to an end but the emphasis lies on the individual family setting about the task in its own way and in its own style. Although the approach is somewhat more relaxed, a more prescriptive model may be appropriate to meet particular needs.

Parents of handicapped adolescents have had very little help in the past and may well have become accustomed to their isolation from professionals. By the time their child is ready to leave school, some parents have come to accept a role as permanent caretakers, just as some adolescents have largely accepted a role of passivity. Parents of adolescents and young adults have often reached a modus vivendi and a quality of adjustment to their situation which needs to be respected and which is in any case not easily changed. Many families are resistant to procedures and programmes which emphasise their difference from other families - e.g. visits from professionals, membership of societies, the arrival of special transport at their door. "In our attempts to 'normalise' adolescents, we run the risk of 'denormalising' the family" (Jeffree, 1980).

The period of school leaving marks a critical point in the life of the family as well as that of the adolescent. But although there is now a considerable literature about parents of younger handicapped children, very little is known about families of handicapped adolescents and young adults. How far do such families have special and distinctive needs? To what extent do the roles of parents of handicapped adolescents differ from the role of parents of younger children, both those who are handicapped and those who are not? What kind of services do families need to help them to fulfil their role?

Our working assumption is that the main role of parents of handicapped adolescents if fundamentally the same as that of parents of any other adolescents - to provide a loving and secure home and to prepare them to live independently in the community.

Ordinary families carry out this role in a variety of ways; some do so explicitly and overtly, others more implicitly or by providing models which they hope the young person will follow. We have relatively little information on how families normally perceive their role or carry out their task of preparing for independent living. We do know that they can draw on the experience of their friends and family and that the final outcome is one in which their son or daughter becomes independent and leaves the parental home.

But this is not generally the outcome if the child is severely handicapped. Such families may expect to have to continue to provide a home indefinitely or until circumstances make it impossible for them to continue to do so. Clearly each family will differ in its expectations of the handicapped adolescent and in particular of the extent to which he or she can live independently in the community. These expectations may not necessarily coincide with those of professional staff involved.

FAMILIES' NEEDS AND ATTITUDES

It is all too easy to generalise about 'the needs of families' and to overlook the enormous range of individual differences. These will differ as much as, if not more than, the needs of any other families. We should also beware of drawing too sharp a distinction between parents of handicapped and non-handicapped people. For example, in studying the families of cerebral palsied children, Hewett (1970) concluded that "families meet the day to day problems that handicap creates with patterns of behaviour that in many respects deviate little from the norms derived from studying the families of normal children. They have more similarities with ordinary families than differences from them". Most families of handicapped people have also had several other normal children; the mentally handicapped child is often the last born in the family (46 per cent in both Moncrieff, 1966, and Cheseldine and Jeffree, 1980). Thus many parents will have considerable experience not only of child rearing, but also of helping their older children to achieve independence.

To stress the essential normality of the families is not to deny the range and severity of the problems they face; rather it is to counter the assumptions and sterotypes which have so often been used by professionals and researchers about the underlying social pathologies to be found in the families. Kew (1975) called them 'handicapped families'. The danger lies in the consequent lack of appropriate action by professionals in response to families' needs. For example, parents seeking help at an early stage report being labelled 'over-anxious' and denied credit for close observation of their child (e.g. Schaefer, 1979). Families seeking residential care for their handicapped member may be investigated for 'guilt' and 'rejection'; those not seeking relief may be labelled 'over-protective'. The behaviour of the families may be interpreted as abnormal whatever they do (Wilkin, 1979). It is interesting to note in this context the explanation suggested by Fox, 1974, for his questionnaire finding of increased levels of 'hysteria' in parents of handicapped children: A facility for brashness, over-dramatisation, and a refusal to be intimidated by authority or status, have become necessary for obtaining the best from our services".

The brothers and sisters of handicapped people have also been portrayed as a group very much at risk emotionally, and institutionalisation was (and may still be) recommended "for the sake of the normal children". McMichael (1971) and Kew (1975) suggested that up to a quarter of siblings had moderate to severe problems in adjusting to the situation of handicap. However, these and similar studies were conducted on families who were already receiving help from professional agencies. The few researchers who have talked to the siblings themselves reflect a picture of generally good adjustment by siblings, who mention positive aspects as well as drawbacks (e.g. Grossman, 1972; Grailiker et al.; 1962). Extra burdens tend to be reported particularly for older sisters, who may be expected to share the increased daily tasks of caring for the handicapped child (Farber, 1959; Fowle, 1968; Gath, 1974; Wilkin, 1979).

The main tradition of British research on the families of handicapped people has been to look pragmatically at daily living problems. Most studies have considered the families of school-age children or younger - a notable exception being Bayley (1973), who interviewed the families of severely handicapped adults living at home. Interview studies in general have had two major drawbacks: the lack of comparative information on families of non-handicapped adolescents and the lack of objective data, for example, through over-dependence on information from parents. However, a number of observations relevant to the families of handicapped young people may be made.

Older studies painted a graphic picture of the financial and housing needs of families. Tizard and Grad (1961) found that 40 per cent of their London sample whose 'severely subnormal child' (aged up to 45 years) lived at home were overcrowded by local standards. Both low income level and overcrowding were somewhat relieved in the comparable sample whose children had been institutionalised. A follow-up of the same families whose handicapped member lived at home found improved housing standards, but greater financial hardship, through more parents being retired or infirm (Moncrieff, 1966). In a more recent study in an urban area, Wilkin (1979) noted that 10 per cent of families he interviewed still had no inside toilet. So the basic housing needs of families caring for a severely handicapped person can still not be said to have been met completely in Britain. Of families interviewed by

Lonsdale (1978), 71 per cent felt their financial circumstances were adequate, but added that unless they had the weekly Attendance Allowance and grants from the Joseph Rowntree Trust many more would be struggling. Poor housing and financial hardship have a consequent bad effect on health, which in turn will be aggravated by the care of a handicapped child (Carnegie United Kingdom Trust, 1964). As the handicapped person grows older, parents' health is likely to become poorer.

Problems of definition affect much of what is said and written about parents' attitudes, felt needs, and reports of their child's behaviour. For example, what types of 'behaviour problems' make the difference between a family being able to keep their handicapped member at home and having to seek an alternative? One study of teachers reported that the most frequent type of behaviour problem was 'non-compliance', but that the most difficult to manage was stereotypic behaviour (Wehman and McLaughlin, 1979). Both types of behaviour may cause embarrassment in public, but the latter may restrict a handicapped young person's possibilities for independent activity more than the former. Even in the older studies of families, management of the behaviour of the handicapped person is cited as the greatest problem - and the one most likely to lead to application for institutionalisation (Tizard and Grad, 1961; Holt, 1958; Bayley, 1973). In our study of mentally handicapped school leavers, 41 per cent of parents mentioned behaviour problems with regard to the young person's leisure time (Cheseldine and Jeffree, 1980). Bayley (1973) estimated that 18 per cent of severely subnormal adults living at home could not be left unsupervised for even an hour.

Several studies that have followed up handicapped young people some years after leaving school strongly suggest that many of them are not only without services but largely isolated from the community resources available to other young people. Even those who can attend some form of day care often lead lonely and unstimulating lives, and have very limited opportunities to make and meet friends or to take part in leisure or recreational activities. Many do not even have access to any form of day care or further training or education; consequently, they are forced to spent most of their time at home and are thrown back on their own resources (Segal, 1971).

On the other hand, we should also note that some of the school leavers in our survey do not present any problems; for example, only 6 per cent were concerned about lack of friends and 46 per cent of the families had no suggestions for ways in which the services could be improved (Cheseldine and Jeffree, 1980). In accounting for these findings, it has to be borne in mind that these families had seen many improvements in services since their child was first born and were often appreciative of the extent to which services had changed for the better. It seems likely that the newer generation of parents of younger children may have higher expectations both of their handicapped children and of the services; in particular, those who have derived benefit from programmes of parent-professional collaboration while their child is at school are likely to press for further working contact with the staff of adult services (Mittler, 1979).

Policies of normalisation for the lives of handicapped people often originated with parent pressure groups. Yet, when it comes to change for their own child, parents may be afraid. With adolescents, parents fear their child being robbed, raped or getting lost. In one study, 40 per cent of severely mentally handicapped adolescents who had left school never went unescorted beyond the front gate (Stanfield, 1973). Parents may identify a lack of companions and proper recreational facilities as problems for handicapped adolescents, and yet tend to keep their own children in familiar company and not trust them out alone. Thus they may undermine the acquisition of skills identified as desirable for the young people by professionals. Ferrara (1979) found that parents of severely handicapped adolescents were more positive about normalisation policies in general than parents of the less severely handicapped. She noted that the degree of personal risk for these parents may be lessened, because their children will require significant adaptations from 'normal' patterns of living to suit their requirements. Boggs (1978) eloquently argues the problems for the severely handicapped: "Rather than trying to create a 'normal' environment for my son, I try to think of how the world must look from his point of view, and what kind of environment would not only minimise his boredom and loneliness, but enhance his sense of dominance".

Thus, parents of handicapped adolescents of all levels of ability may exhibit 'negative parental attitudes' in the face of change. They may just want the best for their child, based on the limited information they have been given, or found out, about their child's abilities and possibilities. "They have seen the reality of what sometimes passes for community care, and no one may have explained to them how things could be otherwise" (Tyne, 1979).

School leaving is therefore a time when information provision and sensitive counselling are vital. Families who find themselves once again caring single-handed for their son or daughter are under considerable stress. The relatively structured existence imposed by the school day and the school year is replaced by one of uncertainty about the future, a situation which also makes considerable day to day demands on the family. It is often necessary for one member of the family (usually the mother) to give up a job in order to look after the handicapped person at home. The loss of income may be a further source of tension in the family as a whole. Furthermore, the less able youngsters may not fully understand why the regular routine of school has suddenly been disrupted or why they are having to spend so much of their enforced leisure at home. The more able young people are even more likely to resent lost opportunities for further education and training; some become bitter and disillusioned; others become unhappy or emotionally disturbed and may even show clinical signs of a depressive illness.

It is therefore ironic that many families are being deprived of services at the very time when they are most in need of them. They need opportunities to discuss their immediate and long-term needs with people who not only know their child but who are also well informed about local existing provision and services that are still being planned. They need to be helped to plan realistically for the future and to prepare the young person step by step to make the best use of whatever services are available. This may mean, for example, preparing him to live away from home, first for a day, then a weekend and then for progressively longer periods. Whether or not he leaves home, they will need continuing help to teach him to become more independent both inside and outside the family home. The extent to which the young person can live in the community will largely depend on the extent to which parents, or parents and professionals in partnership, have succeeded in teaching social independence and community living skills. This we see as one of the most important and distinctive roles of parents and families.

The extent to which the role of families can be realised will therefore depend on many factors which interact with one another in complex ways. The severity of the young person's impairments and disabilities, the opportunities that have been made available in earlier childhood to gain access to appropriate educational and treatment services, the attitudes and perceptions of the young person himself to these efforts - these all play an important part in affecting parents' attitudes to later programmes. Equally critical are the availability of appropriately staffed day or community services which are committed to active programmes of preparation for community living but which include relevant vocational training and further education, as well as help in using community recreational and leisure facilities. Without such services, families are necessarily thrown back on their own resources and are left unsupported to cope with an adolescent who may be physically mature but who is in many respects still dependent on others and in need of skilled programmes designed to help him to take further steps towards social independence.

The following section summarises a number of recommendations that have been made for the kind of service provision which seems to be necessary to meet the needs of parents from the time when their son or daughter is approaching school leaving age.

THE SERVICE NEEDS OF PARENTS

The time of school leaving provides an opportunity to take stock not only of the needs of the child but also those of the family. Families should feel that there is time and opportunity to discuss any aspect of their family life which concerns their child either now or in the future. Such discussions need not be limited to the immediate questions arising from school leaving and placement into adult services. Both parents and professionals are increasingly expressing the wish to move away from a crisis-orientated service towards one which anticipates needs and tries to plan constructively to meet them. For example, parents should be encouraged to discuss questions concerned with residential care long before there is a direct need for it.

Information

First and foremost, parents need information on the range of provision which is available or planned in their in their locality. In our own interviews with parents in areas where services were relatively well developed, we found many parents badly informed about day or residential services for adolescents and adults. Very few had visited the Adult Training Centres which their children would almost certainly be attending in the coming months (Cheseldine and Jeffree, 1980). They were also poorly informed about facilities for short-term and longer-term residential care in their localities. Lack of information was more common among parents who were not members of parent societies or who did not receive the parent journals in which such issues are regularly discussed.

A number of authorities have been producing short information leaflets on local services. These generally contain addresses and telephone numbers of key organisations and individuals as well as useful information on where to get advice or help to meet particular needs. Unfortunately, these leaflets are often aimed at parents of younger children; there is a case for an information sheet written especially for parents of young people approaching school leaving age. This might include information on the following:

    i) local provision for assessment of young people approaching school leaving age - e.g. which professionals should be routinely involved in assessment and decision making and which others are available for consultation if the need should arise?
   ii) procedures for parents to be involved in the process of assessment and decision making; how and when they should be consulted; how they can obtain the information or advice which they feel to be necessary and whom to contact if they are dissatisfied;
  iii) the range of alternative provision which is available locally - e.g. day services, further education colleges, work experience courses, sheltered employment, vocational training. This should include the names of key individuals in these organisations who can advise parents and who might be able to arrange for preliminary visits to the agency;
   iv) the range of residential services - both long-term and short-term - should also be summarised in such a leaflet, together with some indication on how parents can visit such facilities informally.
    v) In addition to listing services for handicapped people, such leaflets should also include information on all relevant resources available to the rest of the community and to young people in particular - e.g. careers advice, work training, further education facilities, evening classes and the whole range of leisure, sport and recreational facilities in the area.

Anticipating needs for residential and support services

Such information leaflets may provide the basis for an informed discussion between parents and professionals on the availability of local resources. For example, parents often express the need not only to be told about the local services that are available or planned but also to have the opportunity to discuss the advantages of the various alternatives in relation to the needs of their son or daughter and of the family as a whole.

Discussion about the range of alternatives may also provide opportunities for families to express more general feelings about their attitudes and needs. To this end, it is obviously desirable that there are opportunities to relate to a single individual, preferably someone with experience of working with families. Such a person can provide the 'single point of contact' recommended by the Warnock Committee in the United Kingdom (Department of Education and Science, 1978). Their role is not merely one of providing information and helping to ensure that services are provided in a co-ordinated manner. It includes the more complex skills involved in helping families to express their anxieties and to discuss matters which are of deep concern to them. Families need time to get to know the visiting professional, to reassure themselves that he or she will come again, and is a person in whom they can have confidence. Only then will they trust themselves to express their deeper needs and feelings. For example, a quick and superficial visit to the family may well result in a report that the family are unwilling to consider residential care. But several visits and the development of a more open and trusting relationship may help the parents to speak more freely about their problems in continuing to provide 24-hour care and may make them less hesitant to express their wish to think about residential care outside the home.

Similarly, some parents may refer to arrangements that have been made for an older brother or sister to make a home for the handicapped youngster when the parents are no longer able to do so. This was mentioned quite frequently in our own studies, particularly as many of the leavers were the youngest of a large family, with many brothers and sisters now married (Cheseldine and Jeffree, 1980). In a separate survey, some 30 per cent of the children in special schools for the mentally handicapped came from families with four or more older children (Mittler and Preddy, 1980). But parents may be reluctant to rely on their other children to take over care, though there is evidence that older siblings no longer living at home tend to give considerable help and are willing to take over. Bayley (1973) found that among mentally handicapped adults living in the community, 85 per cent of those who could be living with a sibling (i.e. both parents dead) were doing so, though of those in hospital, half had been admitted immediately after the death of a parent. But such an arrangement is not necessarily entered into willingly by the older brother or sister or their spouse; it may be made in order to reassure worried parents that the handicapped youngster will be taken care of when the time comes. Furthermore, circumstances can change, particularly in a growing family. For these and other reasons, it is important for the professional not simply to record that family arrangements have been made but to explore the situation in some depth and detail both with the parents and the younger family involved.

In our interviews in the Greater Manchester area, we found few families of school leavers who were well informed about the residential services which were available in their area. Many still assumed that the long-stay mental handicap hospital was the only alternative to remaining at home and were unaware of existing and planned local authority provision for hostels and group homes. The movement towards the use of ordinary housing for handicapped people, although increasingly influential in professional circles, has not made the same impact on individual families.

It has been our experience that parents expect to continue to provide a home for their handicapped son or daughter indefinitely, until they are no longer able to do so by reason of age, incapacity or death. The notion that young people might be given opportunities to live away from their families before there is a crisis has as yet made relatively little headway. This is partly due to the shortage of provision in the community but is also related to the narrow range of alternative accommodation which has until recently been considered appropriate. This may change, now that more consideration is being given to the use of ordinary housing and evidence is beginning to be published indicating that even severely handicapped people can live in ordinary houses. The amount and nature of the support they will need will obviously vary from person to person. In the field of mental handicap, the scheme developed by the Eastern Nebraska Community Organisation for the Retarded (ENCOR) for a wide range of living units in the community is beginning to become influential in the United Kingsom and in other European countries (e.g. Thomas, Firth and Kendall, 1978; Mittler, 1979a). Furthermore, some advisers are now cautioning against the adoption of oversimplified notions of placement - e.g. that people with certain levels of disability need one form of care, whereas those with lesser degrees of disabilities need another (Development Team for the Mentally Handicapped, 1980). Instead, current thinking emphasises the possibility of developing small homes for groups who are not necessarily homogeneous in terms of severity of handicap, though such a policy is clearly not without problems. Nevertheless, it seems useful to counter the prevalent assumption that some people are inevitably 'hospital' cases, while others are 'hostel' or 'group home' cases. Such predictions are likely to be self-fulfilling, and need to be questioned by professionals and parents alike.

The notion that each community should provide homes in the locality for all its handicapped citizens is only now beginning to be seriously discussed. Professionals have come to accept that the number of handicapped people who actually require specialised long-term residential services in hospitals or other institutions is very small; furthermore, studies of such institutions have shown that their resources are often so limited that such specialist needs are rarely adequately met (e.g. Oswin, 1978; Development Team for the Mentally Handicapped, 1980). In the United Kingdom at least, well over four-fifths of severely mentally handicapped children and about a half of the adults are living in ordinary houses with their families; such houses may require a range of adaptations to meet the needs of people with severe physical handicaps but many countries are now developing legislative and financial provision for this purpose.

Providing ordinary or adapted housing in the local community means that people can live in small units, with as much staffing and support as their individual needs require. Some will require only a very occasional visit from a social worker, health visitor or voluntary worker; other houses may contain three to five more dependent people who will need to have staff living in the house with them; in other cases, professional staff live in a nearby house but are available when needed. The emphasis in such schemes is on providing a wide range of residential accommodation to meet the wide range of need of individuals.

From the parents' point of view, such arrangements provide ideal opportunities to help their sons and daughters to learn to live more independently. At the same time they can prepare themselves to accept that, although they will eventually need to live away from home, such a home need not be a distant hospital or institution but a house not very far away from their own.

Quite apart from questions concerned with long-term residential care, families also need opportunities to discuss questions concerned with short-term care in their area. Although hospitals have traditionally made the major contribution to short-term care in Britain, particularly during the summer holidays or in emergencies, local authorities and voluntary organisations have also begun to make provision (see National Development Group, 1977, for a summary of suggestions on how short-term care might be organised at local level). Here again, families may be unaware of these developments and still assume that short-term care is available in hospital or not at all.

Many families will need some short-term relief from the strain of coping. Play schemes during school holidays, and occasional care at the weekends are seen as the most strongly felt needs of parents of younger children (e.g. Barnardo's, 1979). Wilkin (1979) makes the point that it may be important to ask what a family would "like", because he found that mothers were not inclined to identify "need" if they were actually coping. In his study of severely handicapped children at home, 68 per cent of families felt the need of minding in the school holidays (48 per cent said it was "very important"), 48 per cent felt the need for some day care at weekends, 40 per cent for help with 'baby sitting' in the evenings, and 51 per cent needed help with transport (p. 192). However, Lonsdale (1978) reported that 45 per cent of the parents she interviewed considered short-term hostel care unnecessary and would never place a child of theirs in one. They relied in emergency on the family circle and would not "put the child away", though this attitude may be related to the age of the child, Lonsdale's sample being only up to 12 years of age. Some parents seem to fear the loss of a companion, if the young person is more independent. It is often reported that young handicapped people lack friends and contacts outside the family; this isolation may have affected the whole family as well as the handicapped member (Holt, 1958; Boruchow and Espenshade, 1976).

Financial Help

Many countries are now introducing a range of financial grants and allowances both to families and to the handicapped person. The whole question of disability allowances is generally extremely complex and difficult to understand, and parents will almost always need to have access to sources of expert advice. Some cities in the United Kingdom have therefore appointed a welfare officer specifically for disabled persons and their families. This person is independent of the authorities and seeks to ensure that all families obtain the full range of benefits to which they are entitled. Even where such an appointment is not made, clearly written information leaflets are obviously needed, together with suggestions on how further information can be obtained at local level. Here again, these questions need full discussion between parents and professionals.

Information and opportunities for full and informal discussion between parents and professionals constitute essential foundations for any locally based service. But recent thinking also emphasises that much can be achieved by the development of a more active working partnership between parents and professionals in helping the young person to learn to live more independently in the community. The following section examines the nature of such a partnership in greater detail and outlines some of the obstacles to its achievement.

PARTNERSHIP BETWEEN PARENTS AND PROFESSIONALS

Partnership with parents is now seen as the hallmark of a good service for handicapped children. Starting at the time when the handicap is first identified, continuing through pre-school and into the period of formal schooling, partnership between parents and professionals is seen as making a major contribution to meeting the needs of children, parents and professionals alike. The available evidence suggests that handicapped children will respond more favourably to teaching and developmental programmes if parents and professionals are working together than if either is working in isolation (Cunningham, 1975). This is true not only of handicapped children but applies also to those who are 'socially disadvantaged'. The nature of the partnership will vary from family to family and will depend on the needs of the child but a number of elements can be distinguished:

i) involvement of parents in the comprehensive assessment of the child's abilities and disabilities, strengths and needs. Clearly, the parents' knowledge of what their child can and cannot do is invaluable to the teacher. This is particularly true of the more severely handicapped children for whom parents and teachers will share similar goals - e.g. in teaching self-care and social independence skills.

ii) arising directly from joint assessment, teachers and parents can benefit greatly by collaborating in drawing up long-term and short-term goals and in discussing how they are going to work together to help the young person to reach those goals.

The kind of collaboration which we envisage between parents and professionals ideally calls for a home visiting or domiciliary service. This is not intended to replace visits to the school or agency by parents but rather to complement it. A home visiting service is even more essential where the handicapped person is not regularly attending any form of day service; in such cases the main responsibility for helping parents to provide teaching and other forms of training falls on the home visitor.

Examples of such a home visiting service for parents of pre-school children can be found in the Portage programme developed initially in rural areas in the United States but now successfully replicated in the Caribbean and in parts of Europe (Shearer and Shearer, 1972; Revill and Blunden, 1978, 1980). The model here is one in which a home visitor visits families about once a week in order to work with the parent to select short-term goals and to introduce specific structured methods which the parent can use to try to teach the child to reach such goals before the next visit. Although the teaching targets would require considerable modification for adolescents and their families, the model of a home visiting service in which agreed goals are taught could well be found useful by parents and professionals. It might, for example, be used by peripatetic instructors based on Adult Training Centres, as suggested by staff themselves in a national survey (Whelan and Speake, 1977).

Even where the young person is not in regular contact with professionals, parents can be given the means to try to develop active teaching methods which are designed to help the young person learn new skills and to become more independent. Our colleagues Edward Whelan and Barbara Speake have written a teaching manual specifically for parents of mentally handicapped adolescents (Whelan and Speake, 1979). Beginning with a 'Scale for Assessing Coping Skills', parents are helped to complete a simple check list of the young person's abilities in the areas of self-help (personal, domestic, community), social academic (e.g. telling the time, communication, money) and interpersonal (e.g. conversation, friendship, sexual knowledge and behaviour). Detailed suggestions are then made for ways in which parents can design and carry out a teaching programme to help the young person achieve specific skills. Such an approach can also form the basis of structured workshops in which groups of parents and professionals meet regularly in order to define short-term goals and agree on methods of reaching them.

But although professionals and parents of handicapped children have worked in closer partnership during the past ten years, there are few reports of similar parental involvement in services for handicapped adolescents and young adults. Are there distinctive problems about developing such a working relationship between parents of adolescents and adults and the staff who work with them?

Parents frequently complain that they are not involved in the process of decision making about their son or daughter. For example, when there are case conferences to discuss future placement after leaving school, parents may be left to wait outside while the discussion is proceeding among professionals and are only invited in to comment on a decision that has already been formulated. This is less likely to happen if parents and teachers have worked together during the school years in developing joint assessments of the child's abilities and in collaborating on programmes of teaching. But parents of the oldest children in a school may not be as familiar with such an approach since this has often only been developed in recent years and with parents of younger children. They may therefore need more encouragement to involve themselves in discussion and decision making about the future.

Because parents and professionals may not have the same goals, it is important to provide opportunities for a free discussion to identify expectations of the level of independence that may be achieved, since these may differ widely in both groups. Just as several professionals working with the same adolescent may have different expectations of the final outcome, so different members of the same family may vary considerably in their estimate of the extent to which the young person can learn the skills to live successfully in the community. It may therefore be helpful to explore these questions through discussion. It is clearly dangerous to press ahead with carefully structured training programmes to teach social independence when one or both parents may have misgivings about whether such a programme is justified. They may also be anxious about the risks involved in undertaking it. Questions concerned with sexuality represent the most obvious examples where full discussion about goals and philosophies is important. Similarly, parents and professionals may have different perceptions about the extent to which a particular youngster is 'ready' to start a course of social independence training - e.g. in learning to use public transport, go to a supermarket or a disco unaccompanied, to go on holiday with a group of friends, etc.

Even where parents and professionals are apparently agreed on the overall programmes for social independence training, difficult issues arise when it comes to discussing the nature and degree of parental participation in such programmes. Although there is now a strong body of evidence which testifies to the effectiveness of intensive parental involvement where teaching programmes with younger children are concerned, is it right to extrapolate these to parents of adolescents and young adults? Even if direct parental involvement in social independence programmes is likely to be beneficial to the adolescent, how appropriate is such detailed involvement from a 'normalisation' point of view? Is it appropriate that parents should know exactly what their son or daughter is doing in the course of their day to day social education or training programmes? Even very much younger children like to maintain separate identities between home and school and tend to fend off well-meaning enquiries from parents about what they have been doing in school. It could be argued that even where such enquiries are not apparently resented and even where parents and professionals are working well together to achieve goals that are in the long-term interest of the adolescent, such a close involvement on the part of the parents may in fact reinforce rather than diminish dependency.

These issues about goals and philosophies are not widely discussed in the literature, nor, we suspect, do they receive as much consideration as they should at the level of the individual family when professionals are beginning to draw up training programmes for handicapped young people. Professionals may themselves need help in facing these issues, for example, group discussion, possibly accompanied by role play may help staff to face some of the delicate and complex issues involved. Clearly, no two families have the same needs but certain general strategies can be discussed within a group. For example, some parental involvement programmes may begin with a fairly intensive and detailed level of training by parents but in the context of a clearly worked out plan to reduce the amount of parental involvement on a step by step basis. This can be done more easily with some programmes than others - e.g. in teaching a young person to travel to a day centre by public transport, the programme would probably consist of gradually 'distancing' the parent from the young person. Similarly, the amount and intensity of supervision in teaching young persons to wash their hair can also be slowly but systematically withdrawn.

Now that parents are being asked to enter into detailed and often day to day working partnerships with professional staff in teaching their son or daughter to acquire specific skills, it is particularly important to provide opportunities for them to express their feelings about any difficulties they may be experiencing in working in a teaching role. Some parents quite understandably find such work both demanding and stressful but may find it hard to admit to this, for fear of being thought unco-operative or not 'good parents'. They need to be encouraged to be quite open about these matters; parents should not feel forced to undertake demanding programmes of day to day work and should be able to express their feelings about these matters, preferably to someone who is seen as helpful and in whom they can feel confidence.

Obstacles to Parent-professional Collaboration

Although collaboration between parents and professionals has made considerable gains during the past ten years or so, it is as well to recognise the serious obstacles which stand in the way of further progress in this direction. We will briefly list some of these, distinguishing between those primarily relevant to professionals or to parents. We also refer to some recommendations which have been made to try to increase collaboration. These are based on an invited paper prepared by one of us for a UNESCO meeting on special education (Mittler, 1979b).

Professionals

i) Lack of discussion and preparation for parental participation in their basic training.
ii) Resistance and anxiety at the prospect of parental involvement in schools and programmes. Problems in coming to terms with parents as partners.

- iii) A tendency to display their expertise and to adopt a didactic and sometimes authoritarian approach to parents.
- iv) Difficulty in sharing their own limitation in knowledge and skill with parents.
- v) Tendency to make excessive demands on parents - e.g. in the form of teaching sessions, record keeping, attending meetings.
- vi) Failure to take account of the variety of needs and the range of variation from one family to another.

Parents

- i) Difficulty in coping with the demands now being made of them by professionals: they may be too busy, too exhausted or too pre-occupied with day to day problems presented by the handicapped person or by problems concerned with poverty, poor housing, unemployment or chronic ill health.
- ii) Problems in reconciling demands made by the handicapped person with the needs of other members of the family - marriage partner, siblings, grandparents.
- iii) Tendency to attribute too much expertise to professionals - e.g. resulting in the assumption that staff will accept full responsibility for training a young person in, say, social and domestic skills.
- iv) Underestimation of the abilities and potential of their child to respond to independence training, possibly due to a history of earlier failure.
- v) Where parents do succeed in collaborating with professionals in achieving goals for the handicapped person, they may tend to undermine 'professional expertise' by displaying competence in the use of techniques and terminology traditionally regarded as the exclusive preserve of professionals.

Suggestions for Increasing Collaboration

- i) All programmes of initial training for teachers and other professional personnel should review the extent to which questions concerned with parental involvement are incorporated into the curriculum.
- ii) Special courses concerned with this subject should be mounted at the in-service and post-experience level. These should review existing information on this subject and provide opportunities for discussion and experiment with a range of approaches to parental involvement in local services.

- iii) Persons with advisory or administrative responsibilities for special education should review the quantity and quality of parental involvement programmes in their own areas and, in doing so, consult with local parents and parent associations.
- iv) A selective bibliography on parent involvement including reports of successful programmes should be prepared in each country and made available to all head teachers, advisers and programme directors.
- v) Programmes of research and development on parental involvement should be encouraged in each country.
- vi) Appropriate parent organisations at national levels should be invited to submit their views on parental involvement in school and other service programmes and to put forward suggestions for new developments in this area.

CONCLUSIONS

We have argued that the role of parents of handicapped adolescents is not fundamentally different from that of any other family, namely - to provide a loving and secure home and to prepare them to live as independently as possible in the community. But parents face many difficulties in carrying out this role and are seldom given adequate support or practical help at what is often a difficult time. The needs of each family will obviously differ greatly depending on the problems presented by the adolescent and the parents' perception of how far the ultimate goal of independent living in the community is a realistic one.

These and many other issues need discussion at some depth between parents and professional staff who may have different perceptions of the present abilities of the adolescent and the extent to which he or she can become more competent and independent. We have argued for the development of a close working partnership between parents and professionals, similar in some respects to that being developed with parents of younger children but differing to the extent that the young person is or will soon be legally adult, with the rights and responsibilities that go with adult status. If the goal of training and rehabilitation is the maximum degree of independence, equal partnership between parents and professionals will be needed to define goals and how they can be reached. For example, it is often necessary to develop detailed step by step programmes to help the young person to become more socially mobile, by using public transport and going to places of entertainment.

This may arouse a considerable degree of anxiety if the parents feel that the young person is not yet ready for this kind of training and that harm may be done by pressing too hard and too early. On the other hand, it may also happen that professionals are criticised by parents for setting too low a standard and for not developing a regime of demand and expectation.

Partnership between parents and professionals can take many forms, but certain elements can be clearly distinguished at the time of school leaving. Parents should be fully involved in the process of assessment of strengths and needs and should be seen as full members of the multi-disciplinary team, participating in detail in contributing their unique knowledge of their child's abilities and needs and in making decisions on how these can most appropriately be met locally. To this end, parents will need to have full information on local facilities already available or planned. Following this, parents and professionals can try to work together to plan and implement a programme which aims to help the young person to learn new skills, and to become more independent, and to use an increasing range of community resources and facilities. But parents also need to be able to express any doubts they may have about the ability of the young person to learn to live more independently and to discuss any anxieties they may have about the future, particularly where questions of alternative systems of residential care are concerned.

But the most important contribution has to come from the handicapped adolescents themselves. Although parents and professionals may work well together and be agreed about short-term and long-term goals and methods of achieving them, it is essential to involve the young people themselves to the greatest possible extent by encouraging them to express their own views and by giving them as much information as possible on which to make informed choice. Parents and professionals may, singly or in combination, assume that they 'know what is best' or that the young people are not in a position to express their own views. But even severely handicapped adolescents have shown themselves capable of expressing choice and an informed opinion and made it quite clear that they have a right to be consulted. Some mentally handicapped people have organised their own conferences or attended professional conferences in order to talk about their experience of the services being provided and their wishes for more opportunities to contribute to decisions which will affect their everyday lives.

People living in residential care have begun to insist on a greater degree of participation and are increasingly objecting to the lack of consultation in the running of both day and residential services. When their opinions are sought, it often becomes apparent that they do not by any means agree with the goals which either professionals or parents themselves have set for their future.

Where the aims of parents and professionals do coincide with those of the young people, the resulting programme is likely to be all the more successful and satisfying.

REFERENCES

Barnardo's Salford Project Report. Bolton, Lancs, 1979.

Bayley, M. Mental Handicap and Community Care, London, Routledge and Kegan Paul, 1973.

Boggs, E.M. "Who is putting whose head in the sand, or in the clouds, as the case may be?", in A.P. Turnbull and H.R. Turnbull (eds.) Parents Speak Out: Views from the Other Side of the Two-Way Mirror. Ohio, Charles Merrill, 1978.

Boruchow, A.W. and Espenshade, M.E. "A socialisation programme for mentally retarded young adults", Mental Retardation, 14(1), 1976, pp. 40-42.

Carnegie United Kingdom Trust. Handicapped Children and Their Families. Dunfermline, Carnegie U.K. Trust, 1964.

Cheseldine, S.E. and Jeffree, D.M. "Severely mentally handicapped adolescents: a survey of abilities", (unpublished paper), Hester Adrian Research Centre, Manchester Univeristy, 1980.

Cooper, V. "Training for Employment", in A. Wynn Jones (ed.) What about the Retarded Adult? Taunton: NSMHC (SW Region), 1978.

Cunningham, C.C. "Parents as Educators and Therapists", in C.C. Kiernan and P. Woodford (eds.) Behaviour Modification with the Severely Retarded. Amsterdam: Associated Scientific Publishers, 1975.

Department of Education and Science. Special Education Needs. Report of the Committee of Enquiry into the Education of Handicapped Children and Young People (Chairman: Mrs. M. Warnock), Cmnd 7212, London: HMSO, 1978.

Development Team for the Mentally Handicapped. Second Annual Report 1978-1979. London: HMSO, 1980.

Farber, B. "Effects of a severely retarded child on family integration", Monographs of the Society for Research in Child Development, 25, 1 serial no. 75, 1959.

Ferrara, D.M. "Attitudes of parents of mentally retarded children toward normalisation activities", American Journal of Mental Deficiency, 84, 1979, pp. 145-151.

Fleming, I. "Mentally handicapped school-leavers - their assessment and placement", Apex, 6, 1978, pp. 23-26.

Forder, A. Concepts in Social Administration. London: Routledge and Kegan Paul, 1974.

Fowle, C.M. "The effect of the severely retarded child on his family", American Journal of Mental Deficiency, 73, 1968, pp. 468-473.

Fox, A.M. They Get This Training but They Don't Know How You Feel. Horsham, Sussex: National Fund for Research into Crippling Diseases, 1974.

Gath A. "Sibling reactions to mental handicap: a comparison of the brothers and sisters of mongol children", Journal of Child Psychology and Psychiatry, 15, 1974, pp. 187-198.

Grailiker, B.V., Fishler, K. and Koch, R. "Teenage reaction to a mentally retarded sibling", American Journal of Mental Deficiency, 66, 1962, pp. 838-843.

Grossman, F.K. Brothers and Sisters of Retarded Children: An Exploratory Study, New York: Syracuse University Press, 1972.

Hewett, S. The Family and the Handicapped Child. London: Allen and Unwin, 1970.

Holt, K. "The home care of severely retarded children", Pediatrics, 22, 4, 1, 1958, pp. 744-755.

Humes, C.W., Adamczyk, J.S., and Myco, R.W. "A school study of group counselling with educable retarded adolescents", American Journal of Mental Deficiency, 74, 1969, pp. 191-195.

International Leagues of Societies for the Mentally Handicapped. Step by Step: Implementation of the Rights of Mentally Retarded Persons. Brussels: ILSMH, 1978.

Jeffree, D.M. Personal communication, 1980.

Jeffree, D.M. and Cheseldine, S.E. *Junior Interest Profile*. Manchester: Hester Adrian Research Centre, 1980.

Kew, S. *Handicap and Family Crisis: A Study of the Siblings of Handicapped Children*. London: Pitman, 1975.

Lonsdale, G. "Family life with a handicapped child: the parents speak", *Child: Care, Health and Development*, 4, 1978, pp. 99-120.

McMichael, J.K. *Handicap: A Study of Physically Handicapped Children and Their Families*. London: Staples Press, 1971.

Mittler, P. "Patterns of partnership between parents and professionals", *Parents' Voice*, 29, 1979, pp. 10-12.

Mittler, P. *People not Patients: Problems and Policies in Mental Handicap*, London: Methuen, 1979a.

Mittler, P. "Parents as partners in the education of their handicapped child". Discussion paper presented to meeting on Special Education, UNESCO, Paris, 1979b.

Mittler, P. and Preddy, D. "Mentally handicapped pupils and school leavers", in B. Cooper (ed.) *Handicaps and Needs of Mentally Retarded Children*. New York and London: Academic Press, 1980.

Moncrieff, J. *Mental Subnormality in London: A Survey of Community Care*. London: Political and Economic Planning, 1966.

National Development Group for the Mentally Handicapped. *Residential short-term care: suggestions for action*. London: Department of Health and Social Security (Pamphlet 4), 1977.

O'Dell, S. "Training parents in behaviour modification: a review", *Psychological Bulletin*, 81, 1974, pp. 418-433.

Oswin, M. *Children Living in Long Stay Hospitals*. London: Spastic International Medical Publications and Heinemann, 1978.

Reiter, S. "Vocational counselling of mentally handicapped adults". Unpublished doctoral thesis: Manchester University, 1975.

Revill, S. and Blunden, R. *Home Training of Pre-School Children with Developmental Delay: Report of the Development and Evaluation of the Replication of* the Portage Service in Ceredigion Health District, Dyfed. Cardiff: Mental Handicap in Wales - Applied Research Unit. Research Report No. 5, 1978.

Revill, S. and Blunden, R. A Manual for Implementing a Portage Home Training Service for Developmentally Handicapped Pre-School Children. Windsor: NFER Publishing Company (in press), 1980.

Ryba, K.A. and Brown, R.I. "An evaluation of personal adjustment training with mentally retarded adults", British Journal of Mental Subnormality, 25 (49), 1979, pp. 56-66.

Schaefer, N. Does She Know She's There? London: Futura Publications Ltd., 1979.

Schalock, R.L. and Harper, R.S. "Placement from community-based mental retardation programs; how well do clients do?", American Journal of Mental Deficiency, 83, 1978, pp. 240-247.

Segal, S. From Care to Education. London: Heinemann Medical Books, 1971.

Shearer, M.S. and Shearer, D.E. "The Portage Project: a model for early childhood education", Exceptional Children, 39, 1972, pp. 210-217.

Stanfield, J.S. "Graduation: what happens to the retarded child when he grows up?", Exceptional Children, April, 1973, pp. 548-552.

Swann, W. and Mittler, P. "A survey of language abilities in ESN(S) children", Special Education: Forward Trends, 3, 1976, pp. 24-27.

Thomas, D., Firth, H. and Kendall, A. ENCOR - a way ahead. London: Campaign for the Mentally Handicapped, 1978.

Tizard, J. and Grad, J.G. The Mentally Handicapped and Their Families. Maudsley, Monographs 7. London: Oxford University Press, 1961.

Tyne, A. "Parents are our biggest obstacle", Campaign for the Mentally Handicapped Newsletter, No. 19, 1979, pp. 7-8.

UNESCO, "Expert Meeting on Special Education, Final Report". Paris: UNESCO, 1979.

Wehman, P. and McLaughlin, P.J. "Teachers' perceptions of behaviour problems with severely and profoundly handicapped students", Mental Retardation, 17, 1979, pp. 20-21.

Whelan, E. and Speake, B. _Adult Training Centres in England and Wales: report of the first national survey_. Manchester: National Association of Teachers for the Mentally Handicapped and Hester Adrian Research Centre, University of Manchester, 1977.

Whelan, E. and Speake, B. _Learning to Cope_. London: Souvenir Press, 1979.

Wilkin, D. _Caring for the Mentally Handicapped Child_. London: Croom Helm, 1979.

Zisfein, L. and Rosen, M. "Personal adjustment training: a group counselling program for institutionalized mentally retarded persons", _Mental Retardation_, 11, 1973, pp. 16-20.

Zisfein, L. and Rosen, M. "Effects of a personal adjustment training group counselling program", _Mental Retardation_, 12, 1974, pp. 50-53.

VIII. ALTERNATIVES TO WORK FOR THE HANDICAPPED

By Professor Jack Tizard and
Dr. Elizabeth Anderson,
Thomas Coram Research Institute, London

At an early stage in the project the late Professor Tizard and Dr. Anderson wrote a paper of which we here print an extract. Many participants in the project and contributors to seminars were strongly of the opinion expressed in Part One that any dilution of the principle that those with handicaps had the same rights to work as all citizens was wrong. Nevertheless, the availability of employment is uncertain, particularly for young people, and where the principle cannot be realised in practice alternative life styles need to be sought. It is with this in mind that this edited extract has been included.

One reason why the question of alternatives to work for the handicapped has been neglected is that, in the majority of cases the problem does not present itself as acute and immediate at the time of school-leaving. At this stage, many of those who do not go directly into open or sheltered employment go on to some form of further education or training (provided either in ordinary or special institutions), or, in a minority but increasing number of cases, to bridging courses of some kind. As was the case at school, the assumption is that after a period of training these young people will eventually find employment. The problem is therefore postponed for one or even several years, during which the anxieties of the young people and their parents are temporarily allayed. Thus only for a minority, in most developed countries, is the problem of finding an alternative to work one that must be faced immediately after leaving school.

For those who cannot or do not wish to obtain open or sheltered employment, a number of traditional alternatives exist. Their exact nature, the providers of the services and their availability, differ considerably from one country to another, and also in different parts of the same country.

The main alternative ways of life open to those unable to obtain paid employment vary from one OECD country to another. In many countries the most common alternative is for disabled people, especially young people, to continue to live with their parents, or, increasingly, as more purpose-built housing and better support services become available, in their own homes, and then to go out to some kind of day centre, for example some kind of "training" or "work" or "occupational" centre. A much less common alternative is to live in a residential institution, often specifically for the handicapped and either to use its own facilities or to go out to a local day centre during the day. A third possibility is to build up a life based on the family home, or one's own home, and on the local community, rather than regularly attend some form of day provision. While these three ways of living are all fairly common, all kinds of variations on them are possible. A disabled person may, for example, go out to some sort of organised provision once or twice a week, and build up a life for him- or herself based on the home (perhaps including occasional part-time home-based employment) during the rest of the week.

A person's preferred life-style is likely to change with age. A young person might, after leaving school, first attend some type of day provision, then might marry and decide to stop work and to devote his time and energies to looking after the home and his spouse, thus building up as independent a life in the home as possible. Today there is often a feeling among school leavers and their families that once a "placement" has been found for them in a "training centre" or its equivalent, they are there "for life". This may have been the case in the past (if such provision existed at all) but is becoming less and less likely.

We have just suggested that the most commonly used organised "alternative" to work available for severely handicapped young people, at least for those living in urban areas, is some sort of day provision. In the United Kingdom, for example, such provision is of two main types. These overlap, and each encompasses a number of variants, but generally, provision for mentally handicapped young people is made in Adult Training Centres (now being renamed "Social Education Centres") and for the physically handicapped in "day" or (a term now falling out of use) "occupational" centres. Many though not all western countries have equivalents to these forms of provision. Often they are of fairly recent origin, and in some countries they are only available in large centres of population.

Two major questions arise in relation to special forms of provision such as these. The first is whether provision of this kind is something which countries should be aiming to set up (or, if it already exists, to maintain in its present form); the second is how the quality of such provision, where it does exist, can be improved.

The reason for posing the first of these questions is that centres which cater for special groups such as "the physically handicapped", "the mentally handicapped", "the elderly", tend to be segregative in their effects, whatever their intentions. Suggestions are made later about how such a tendency can be counteracted, but a strong case could be made for saying that these suggestions are merely palliatives, and that the whole concept of centres for particular groups (for example severely physically handicapped young adults) is wrong.

Even if one does not accept this argument, and believes that there is a real need, at least for some severely handicapped school leavers and young adults, for special day facilities, it is generally agreed that there is often considerable confusion about the aims of such centres, in particular about the relative importance in them to be given to social education, vocational training, further education, creative and recreational activities and to "work". These problems, together with the views of both users and providers of services, are discussed later in this report.

In many countries, more attention has been paid to the quality of day provision for the mentally handicapped than for the physically and multiply handicapped. In the United Kingdom, for example, the Secretary of State for Social Services set up in 1975 the National Development Group for the Mentally Handicapped, an independent advisory body whose terms of reference were "to advise on the development and implementation of better services for mentally handicapped people and their families." Their pamphlet on day services(7) provides a useful summary of the present situation with suggestions for improvements in day provision. The emphasis is still however very much on training for eventual employment, and comparatively little thought has been given to the lot of those who are unlikely to obtain work.

For young physically and multiply handicapped leavers, the nature and quality of day provision is extremely variable. Thus in Britain, until recently, in many areas day centres catered mainly for elderly people, and a severely physically handicapped school leaver might find himself in a centre where the vast majority of clients were in their sixties and seventies. More recently however there has been a trend towards setting up more centres geared to the needs of physically and multiply handicapped adolescents and young adults. An unusual form of provision for the physically disabled is the Day Work Centres run by the U.K.

Spastics Society, which cater for nearly 1,000 clients, three-quarters of whom are under the age of 30. They are unique in that although they provide for youngsters considered "unemployable", and eligible for welfare benefits, they are totally work-oriented.

While living at home and going out to day provision is very common, quite large numbers of young people, especially those who are severely handicapped - fall into the second main group referred to above, that is, they live in residential institutions (usually specifically for the handicapped and often set up by voluntary organisations) or are in long-term hospital care. Some of these young people go out daily to day centres of the kinds described above; for others alternatives to work are available where they are living. The problems of finding satisfying ways of using the "working day" are similar to those of the young people who live at home and go out to day centres, although there is a much greater danger that the residents of institutions will become segregated from the ordinary life of the community.

Oswin(16) has drawn attention to the fact that in many long-stay hospitals for mentally handicapped children and adults there is often one group for whom the quality of life is particularly poor. These are residents whose multiple handicaps make them highly dependent on the staff for their physical care needs. This may lead to their being categorised as "low-grade", and misperceived as people for whom the activities in or outside the hospital organised for the "higher-grade" residents (which may be excellent and imaginative) are considered inappropriate. Many such young adults may even continue to live in children's wards until their late twenties because of over-crowding in adult wards. Oswin suggests that even where a person is so severely handicapped that he cannot, for example, use his hands at all, or communicate except in the most restricted way, the benefit and enjoyment he gets from observing what others do must not be underestimated and he should therefore be included in the full range of activities which that particular institution offers.

As already noted large numbers of severely disabled young people do not only live at home, without paid employment, but spend all or the main part of the working week in their homes. In some countries the main reason for this is simply that very little, if any, day provision exists. In others, for example the United Kingdom, most towns and cities do have some form of day provision but there is little available for those living in rural areas, apart from some experimental mobile day centres(11) or mobile adult training centres(15). Even where some form of provision does exist, many congenitally disabled young people and adults as well as those who become disabled later in life choose to develop, or retain, a life based on their homes.

DO THE CURRENT ALTERNATIVES NEED TO BE CHANGED?

Before looking at innovative ways of providing alternatives to work, the question must be raised as to whether or not, and in what ways, the provision which is already available needs to be changed. That something is wrong seems self-evident even without research findings such as those from the fairly recent (1973) Southampton Servey of all physically disabled people under retirement age in that city(21). This showed that over a quarter of the 1,095 people interviewed were depressed, one-third found their restricted lives lonely, and nearly half worried about some aspect of their struggle to live. These are rather general findings: do we have any more precise information about what the users of centres and the professionals involved in running them or setting them up actually think? Below, several points of view are presented.

We start with some provocative comments made by a severely disabled cerebral-palsied professional man as to whether or not alternatives are needed to the typical adult training centres and work centres of the kinds described earlier. "Perhaps we are all /i.e. disabled and able-bodied professionals/ in danger of instilling our own concept into these kids...I've a pretty good knowledge of the /local/ Adult Training Centres...and I've talked to a lot of the people who attend them. I didn't find one adverse comment, they were all happy and content. I could see what was wrong with them; the staff could, but I couldn't help wondering if we were all of us being arrogant and superior. We all have one life and we talk, those of us who are in the business of talking this way, glibly about 'achieving potential', 'widening horizons', 'achieving a meaningful existence'. Meanwhile the folk we are talking about very often just quietly get on with the idea of being happy. I'm not saying we're wrong: I think we're right. They are happy partly because society has instilled low expectations into them and they are simply playing out their role. But we need to realise, I think, that they must have some right to be happy in that role, and we should perhaps be wary of disturbing them unless we are sure we have something better...". Is he right? Are the majority of users of centres such as these generally contented? Is there a need for change?

Here is another viewpoint. This time the writers are two able-bodied professionals, one co-organiser of a community arts group, the other a teacher and writer.

In a strongly-worded article on Adult Training Centres (ATCs) they refer to a recent United Kingdom television programme which "documented a depressing catalogue of conditions. It showed mentally handicapped workers paid about £2 or £3 for a 27- or 30-hour working week. This is a world where snapping wheels onto toy tractors all day is described as 'of great therapeutic value'... If monkeys were made to do the same work, there would be a national outcry."(6) The authors refer to the fact that "nine out of ten ATCs rely on such contract work", and that "contractors save on pensions, national insurance, welfare and redundancy payments, heating, lighting and the rest. They use ATCs against homeworkers, other sheltered workshops...and against each other, knowing their dependence on their contracts....

Beneath the present complacency about ATCs there seems to be more than the hint of a smug assumption that we are really doing the mentally handicapped a favour by providing ATCs at all. With ATCs we give them self-respect. If it wasn't for ATCs they would either be sitting at home vegetating or have to be in a subnormality hospital."

The authors go on to comment that "our expectations of the mentally handicapped are too low; that most, though they may be slower than other workers, have the ability to work and to work well and, if working, should receive a proper wage rather than depending largely on state benefits; that some of the users of the centres, especially those who have recently left school, realise that ATCs don't provide real work and dislike what they are doing" (they quote remarks such as: "it's boring"; "I hate it"; "you get told off if you can't do enough", which conflict with the findings of the previous writer; that "too few ATCs provide proper training, and only a very small number of trainees go on to open employment; that while many ATCs do try to continue the education of their workers, this is often incompatible with demands made by contract work, so that they are really unsuitable school places for young adults to go to when they leave school."

Many of these, as well as other, criticisms have been expressed in much greater detail in research in the United Kingdom and elsewhere into the functioning of Adult Training Centres or their equivalents, as well as by a variety of groups working on behalf of the mentally handicapped, and, as noted earlier, various suggestions about improvements have been made.(5) Questions which constantly arise in almost all countries are the extent to which training centres or their equivalents should restrict themselves to "training" and education functions (and if so, training and education for what, and for how long? Until the young adult is 25? or 30? Or for "as long as he or she can benefit?"); to what extent they should provide what is, in effect, sheltered work;

whether the two functions can or should be combined; and so on.

Views of the users of special centres

The writers whose views we quoted first were not themselves users of centres so, to obtain more systematic pictures of users' views, we quote from two recent studies which, among other things, attempted to find out what the users in two different types of day centres actually thought about their work.

The first of these is one of the few studies in which mentally handicapped users of centres were asked about their views. It was carried out in the Inner London Borough of Wandsworth in 1974,(5) and involved interviewing 106 users of three Adult Training Centres about their experience in the ATCs and at home. Twenty per cent of those interviewed were considered to be "mildly" mentally handicapped (defined as "potentially employable and able to live unsupervised"), 60 per cent moderately handicapped ("capable of routine social activities like shopping but always likely to need supervision") and 20 per cent as "profoundly" handicapped ("at most, capable of routine physical activities like washing and dressing by themselves; always needing close supervision"). Nearly half fell into the 18-24 year age group. All the trainees were asked a number of general questions, the most important being whether they liked coming to the centre. Only 12 per cent did not like doing so, all were women, and most were moderately handicapped and in the 18-24-year-old age group.

A representative sample of 54 trainees were then asked more detailed questions. One was why they came to the centre; 39 per cent gave variations on the answers "because I like it"; 39 per cent other positive reasons such as to "work" or to learn; 11 per cent avoidance of something worse (e.g. not wanting to stay at home) and 11 per cent did not know. Trainees were also asked what they did at the centre, what they liked best, and what they liked least. The general picture was as follows: trainees saw the centres as places of employment or for other more creative activities. Nearly two-thirds liked the creative activities best /responses included under this heading were reading, writing, painting, games, cooking, hairdressing, etc.7, and only one-quarter preferred the employment activities /sub-contract work7. What was particularly significant was that 38 per cent of the trainees really disliked at least one of the employment activities, the main dislike being towards work on pins and hooks, a kind of industrial subcontract work involving the fitting of wire onto a card. Another significant point to emerge from the study was that although the majority of trainees did like coming to the centre,

76 per cent said that they wanted to get a job outside the centre (in open employment) while only 21 per cent did not want to do so. Only a tiny proportion of trainees had, in the past, in fact moved into open employment, although with the recent opening of a more employment-oriented centre it was hoped that more would do so.

In another study Schlesinger[17] interviewed a 10 per cent representative sample of the cerebral-palsied workers in 26 Spastics Society Work Centres. The centres were almost entirely work-oriented (i.e. sub-contract work): they catered for a predominantly young group (77 per cent were under 30 years old, and 34 per cent straight from school), most of them (74 per cent) living at home. Ninety-eight per cent of the workers had a physical impairment (58.3 per cent mild, 34.5 per cent moderate and 4.8 per cent severe), 60 per cent were mentally handicapped, and 40 per cent had a speech disorder. The majority were multi-handicapped.

Among the findings were the following: 70 per cent of the sample saw themselves as "workers" rather than trainees - one comment for example was: "A Work Centre is a person's work, which should be treated as a serious job", i.e. the Centre's users "are in favour of the present orientation and take pride in regarding themselves as workers." The writer of the report felt, overall, that the centres still offered a unique service for the severely handicapped "most of whom will probably work there permanently because they will never reach outside employment", and commented on the "friendly, happy atmosphere of the centres and the obvious employment of those attending", an impression "supported by the workers' own comments."

However, this was only part of the picture. The survey found that there was much unused potential in the workers since "in the main the jobs that are undertaken do not allow for the full use of workers' abilities, learning of new skills, or a sense of achievement and purpose. In fact, nearly half the workers are rated by managers as under-using their abilities. The general level of task is low, and because work is largely chosen for reasons of economy or availability it rarely reflects the majority interests of those who are doing it, or gives them an opportunity for developing skills such as responsibility and decision making." Although none of the workers stated they were being exploited, they were paid on a similar basis as trainees in Adult Training Centres i.e. up to (and often below) the maximum (£4 a week) consistent with receiving full benefit from social security.

NEW APPROACHES TO SIGNIFICANT LIVING WITHOUT WORK

The evidence presented so far suggests that there is likely to be an increasing need for providing alternatives to work for many groups in the community, including mildly as well as severely handicapped people, and that the existing alternatives are frequently unsatisfactory. In this section we present ideas about the possible content of a meaningful life without work, and make suggestions about how such activities might be organised within the existing framework or provisions, for those (probably a majority) who prefer some structuring of the way in which they spend their day. Although we believe that some of the suggestions made below can, if followed up, help to enhance the quality of life of those living without work, what constitutes a worthwhile and meaningful life must remain a very subjective and personal matter. And as we pointed out earlier, many people, both handicapped and non-handicapped, will continue to feel that they have a "right to work" and that society should accommodate to them, in its provisions and its attitudes, rather than vice versa.

Participation in voluntary work

Earlier it was argued that one of the main functions of work was to provide an individual with a sense of personal worth, and involvement in society at large. A number of handicapped young people and adults believe, as we do, that these needs could be met at least in part by participation in some form of voluntary service. The potential for the involvement of handicapped people as givers rather than receivers of services has hardly begun to be explored; we consider it one of the most fruitful approaches to the question of alternatives to work.

Before making specific suggestions about what handicapped people might wish to do, and outlining innovative schemes, we want to look at the part played by voluntary "work" or "help" or service in improving and maintaining the quality of life in the community as a whole. Many of the points made in the following paragraphs are taken from the 1978 U.K. Wolfenden Report(24) on the future of voluntary organisations.

In the Wolfenden Report four main sectors were identified as involved in meeting social and other needs. Their relative importance will of course vary greatly from one country to another. The four sectors include: (a) the statutory services (which, despite their obvious advantages, have in all societies certain disadvantages, e.g. they are costly, bureaucratic and may seem formal and remote); (b) the commercial or market system of provision; (c) voluntary organisations; (d) the "informal network of support provided by family, friends and neighbours". The dividing lines between the latter two, with which we are particularly concerned, are frequently of course very blurred, and their importance in the total network of provision difficult to estimate, although almost certainly underestimated.

We consider first organised voluntary help. The role of voluntary organisations tends to differ from that of statutory bodies in that they act as pressure groups, as pioneers, as providers of alternative or complementary services or sometimes as sole providers of a service. Large numbers of volunteers are involved; for example, a National Opinion Poll held in the United Kingdom in 1976 suggested that about 5 million individuals aged 16 or over had undertaken some voluntary work during the past year (average total was six hours) under the auspices of a voluntary or statutory organisation. In two typical British towns with populations of around 50,000, 4 per cent of the population were actively engaged in voluntary work, catering in particular for children and young people and, to a much lesser extent, for the elderly. Significant trends include "the re-orientation of some organisations to provide more specialised help; the rapid growth of pressure groups involved with poverty, housing, disability, etc. and of mutual help groups (e.g. pre-school, play-groups); the growth of co-ordinating bodies and the increasing encouragement by local and central government of voluntary organisations."

Turning next to the informal system of social helping, the small amount of evidence which does exist suggests that the volume of such help is even greater than that of organised voluntary help, and that if it ceased an enormous burden would be placed on other systems of provision. According to the Wolfenden Report, the informal system contributes particularly in the provision of care for "the young and the weak", especially the sick, the handicapped and the elderly, and in the provision of advice and psychological support from the experienced to the inexperienced in such matters as child rearing and coping with crises such as divorce, desertion or bereavement. Whereas voluntary organisations tend to attract a disproportionate number of professional and managerial people, the informal network's "volunteers" are drawn from all social groups.

A general trend noted in the Wolfenden Report was the "strong evidence of increasing voluntary activity... particularly in those /organisations/ concerned with young volunteers". A National Opinion Poll Survey showed that those aged 16 to 24 took part in voluntary work as frequently as older age groups. They noted that: "in comparison with the past, many more young people are not in full-time employment either because they are in full-time education or because (recently) they are unemployed.

We suspect that their level of participation in voluntary work has increased substantially and could perhaps increase still further".

A final point of interest raised in the Wolfenden Report concerned the question of motivation for voluntary work. The Report recognised that motives may well be mixed: volunteering may give power or social importance, may fill a gap in a person's emotional life, may be a question of banding together for mutual help and support and so on. But, concludes the Report, most people "just want to do what they can to help somebody else. They may act through what we have called the 'informed sector', giving spontaneous help to relatives and neighbours who need it; they may work as volunteers under the statutory sector; or they may be attracted to a voluntary organisation. The point is that there are millions of such people in our society; and one of the most encouraging features...is the growing evidence of this quality in its younger members...Without this contribution the lives of an immense number of our fellow citizens would be the poorer".

Having tried to look at the nature of, and trends in, volunteer activity in society in general, what contribution might handicapped people wish or be able to make? Research evidence from the Schlesinger study suggested that many cerebral-palsied young people who were not in paid employment but attending Spastics Society Work Centres were giving substantial help to those they were living with, whether these were their families or others in residential homes. For example 66.6 per cent mentioned helping with housework, including food preparation, house decoration, small repair jobs, etc.; 26.2 per cent doing errands outside the home (shopping, posting letters, etc.); 21.4 per cent giving general personal help in the home (including baby-sitting, messages on the phone, etc.); 10.7 per cent giving in some way moral support. Other activities mentioned included helping with the housework, helping others with their hobbies and writing or typing letters. Many of these kinds of activities could be used outside the home in voluntary work in the community.

In fact many disabled people have themselves made suggestions to us about participation in voluntary work. One young woman, very severely handicapped by athetoid cerebral palsy writes that a worthwhile life outside a job context "may involve joining the Women's Institute, offering to baby-sit, visit an old person near us, organising a street waste paper collection for Friends of the Earth, meeting the locals in the pub, in fact generally being sociable and concerned. Also the onus is on us to structure our days so that we are as occupied as can be, and yet are free if neighbours like to drop in. (I have always felt that one of my tasks is to be a good listener)." A young man with severe cerebral palsy, whose home is at present a hospital writes: "Work must be satisfying, fulfilling, if it is not to become mere drudgery. This is where most of the conventional sheltered workshops seem to fall down... There is ...I think, lots of scope for doing voluntary work. I do a little - compiling Bible quizzes for the Fellowship of Christian Writers. Money is a great incentive I know, but it counts for a lot if one is seen to be useful. Perhaps a register of voluntary work, to suit different abilities (and disabilities) would help those who are stuck for a job but have the will to do something. We may be able to help other handicapped colleagues, too."

These are among the ideas which individuals have put to us and many more could be added. To give a better idea of how volunteering can work out in practice two more detailed examples are provided below. The first is a scheme which specifically involves mentally handicapped young people and adults as volunteers; the second a case-study of the involvement of the "housebound" (who may or may not be able-bodied) in the provision of neighbourhood care.

"Volunteering" in practice in an Adult Training Centre

The aim of the first scheme, which has been built up over a number of years at an Adult Training Centre, is to involve moderately and severely mentally handicapped trainees (about half of whom also had some degree of physical handicap, for example spina bifida, cerebral palsy, haemophilia) in voluntary work in their local community, if they wish to do so. The details of the scheme have been provided by the organiser of the centre(8) and also by a member of staff from the U.K. Volunteer Centre who has made an as yet unpublished evaluation of it.(10)

Currently the scheme involves about half of the 88 trainees at the Centre. Of those not involved some are relatively new and have not yet been invited to take part, others have been too handicapped for the opportunities available, or are considered insufficiently responsible to cope with the demands, while others choose not to participate. Trainees who wish to participate but are not considered suitable are told the reasons and where possible helped to master the skills required. The volunteers have so far tended to be among the less intellectually impaired; they include some with Down's syndrome, and some who also have fairly severe physical handicaps (e.g. unable to walk unsupported, speech defects, or poor sight). Before they go out the organiser ensures they are capable of doing the jobs they have volunteered for, and over four years only two trainees have had to be withdrawn from schemes. None work alone, but rather in pairs or groups of about four. More able trainees work with those who are less able or less calm, or who need some degree of supervision, and they give each other, particularly the new volunteers, a great deal of support.

The work carried out by the trainees includes a good deal of work with the elderly. Working in the local geriatric hospital (taking the tea trolley round the wards and serving teas) was especially popular and the outside observer of the scheme concluded that the trainees seemed to derive special satisfaction from working with old people. They liked being recognised as "ordinary" people and being genuinely welcomed by ward staff and patients and they liked the old people's display of affection. Also very popular was washing up at two lunch clubs for the elderly, although volunteers would have valued more chances of chatting with the clients. The club organiser found the trainee-volunteer as efficient as other volunteers and they were not perceived as "handicapped" by most of the lunch club members. Other projects included helping at an old people's centre, and at a residential home for the elderly; working with handicapped children in a special school nursery (two trainees) and in a play-group (two trainees); gardening for elderly and infirm people living alone, delivering newsletters and other specific projects. Suggestions made by trainees themselves indicated that they had a special concern for old people.

What are the factors which appear to determine whether a scheme such as this works well? Of central importance (where substantial numbers of volunteers are involved) is the appointment of a co-ordinator of the work. The scheme described above, which developed from small beginnings, was until very recently, run by the Centre's organiser, but because of the time involved a volunteer liaison co-ordinator (an ordinary volunteer) has just been appointed. Her role is to work closely with the staff at the Centre and with prospective recipients of help from the trainee-volunteers; to seek out volunteer opportunities (experience here indicates that most volunteers need very precisely defined, active roles); to match up particular recipients with particular volunteers (this is not necessarily related to intellectual ability), and to provide general support, especially in picking up potential problems at an early stage. Where substantial numbers of volunteers are involved the appointment of a co-ordinator seems essential. Also the provision of a flexible system of transport.

Such schemes are not without dangers; one is that trainees are sometimes suggestible and could easily be exploited: it has to be made clear to them that they are completely free to participate or not, as they wish. Another question is of course that of how much voluntary work should be done, and whether it cuts into other activities (organised, for example, by the centre) which are of more value to the trainees.

Overall, however, the scheme seems to have been most valuable and Freeth's(10) comments are worth quoting: "People too frequently underestimate the practical capabilities and emotional sensitivity of the mentally handicapped. Experience with this group of trainees shows without any doubt that they can play an active and useful part in the community, if given suitable opportunities. They respond very positively to the pleasure they get from volunteering - and, being rather less inhibited than many people, they are more likely to react honestly to being bored or misused... Growth in personal development and confidence is a positive advantage of working as a volunteer, and it was exciting to see the trainees responding to new situations and new contacts, gaining in assurance and often in ability. There is no doubt that they get a lot out of what they do - and that most of the people they helped seemed to benefit as much, if not more."

Volunteering by housebound adults

Although the volunteers described above were in some cases quite severely handicapped they were not housebound. A detailed example of how the housebound (who may or may not be disabled) can also be involved as volunteers is given in a case study made by the Volunteer Centre in the United Kingdom(23). This describes the work and organisation of a project based on the principle that everyone has something to give. Briefly, through the use of a telephone switchboard system, the housebound are involved as volunteers. Since the area (a small town with a population of 16,000) already had a large number of voluntary organisations, the project's main aim was "to link and supplement existing organisations; to provide a channel of communication for needs to be expressed and known about, and, by means of liaison groups, to try and co-ordinate much of the work currently being done by existing bodies."

The scheme, which has one permanent (unpaid) co-ordinator, involves three main categories of volunteer: telephone, transport and visiting volunteers. The linchpin of the scheme is the 56 regular telephone volunteers including "multiple sclerosis and polio sufferers as well as post-natal depression mums and the elderly", each of whom mans a phone from 9 a.m. to 9 p.m. for one day every eight weeks. Also, to ensure continuity, there are volunteer co-ordinators (each on duty for one week out of eight) who "tie up the ends" and provide backup for the duty volunteers. The telephone volunteers, who have been carefully briefed, receive requests for help or advice from organisations and from individuals. They either refer these requests to an appropriate organisation or, more often, contact one of the 200 local volunteers who are prepared, again on a rota basis, to give individual help by providing transport (70-90 such volunteers) or by visiting (about 100 volunteers). The telephone volunteer on duty for the day has a log book for recording calls, help required/offered, action taken, and follow-up; a diary of transport volunteers for each weekday; a duty volunteer's manual; and the card index of "community facilities". The success of the scheme is indicated by the increase in the number of calls received and help given over the first two years of the project's existence.

The scheme described above is one of a growing number of such schemes. Others are more specific, both in the kind of volunteers participating and in the sort of help offered. Disabled people may, for example, offer specialised information and advice to other disabled people through a telephone scheme run on broadly similar lines.

As noted already, the role of the co-ordinator is central, particularly in ensuring continuity, in establishing and maintaining close links with local statutory and voluntary organisations, and in the recruitment, selection, briefing and support of volunteers.

It could be argued that projects such as these may conceal deficiencies in (or reduce) statutory provision, but one of the goals of the project is to act as a pressure group in revealing such deficiencies. It can also be argued that telephone-based projects can reduce face-to-face neighbourhood helping, and this will be detrimental to those without access to a phone. To try to resolve this, the Volunteer Centre's research group is currently investigating ways in which, perhaps through street-based representatives, the project's existing telephone scheme might be used as a back-up resource for stimulating and strengthening informal neighbourhood caring.

Volunteering: the main issues

A number of issues are involved in the use of volunteers. These are discussed at much greater length than it is possible to do here in the U.K. Volunteer Centre's forthcoming paper on voluntary commitment. They include the extent of involvement and the danger of overcommitting people; the provision of adequate support; and the need to investigate exactly what special skills and resources a particular volunteer has to offer. These questions arise whether or not a person is in paid employment and whether or not he or she is able-bodied.

While, clearly, each individual possesses skills or potential skills which are his alone, certain groups in society may also, through shared experience, have skills to offer which others are less likely to possess, and it may be useful to try to identify these. Retired people, for example, are more likely than others to have time, and also more experience of coping with life crises. Parents with handicapped children are often much better able to offer appropriate support and/or practical advice to other such parents than are professionals. Are there particular resources and/or skills which certain handicapped people possess? Time is one resource which nearly all are likely to have although they may not choose to use it in voluntary work. We have already seen that many severely mentally handicapped people enjoy helping and are able to establish good rapport with elderly people. Again, certain handicapped people, for instance among young people with spina bifida, are much more likely to have spent long periods in hospital than most of the population. Does this give them insights and advice to offer which have never been tapped? Because of experience in fighting large or small battles with bureaucracy for certain basic requirements (e.g. a purpose-built flat or the installation of a telephone) others have acquired the very skills needed by pressure groups and political parties.

This leads to the question of the undoubted ability of many disabled people to help others with disabilities. As the Warnock Committee(20) point out (10.128) "few handicapped people are engaged in helping other handicapped people...With the shortage of social and welfare workers of all kinds...there should be plenty of scope for handicapped people to give encouragement and unpaid help to others who are facing problems which they themselves have had to face and overcome. In addition, there should be scope for handicapped people to do things for others who are in great need of practical help (for example those who are paralysed) even if they have not been through the same experience".

In a moment we will have to consider whether such help should be paid or unpaid; what we are concerned with here is the unused potential of many handicapped people. In the United States, for example, many disabled people "hire" others with disabilities as attendants. The late Donna McGwinn, who was severely handicapped by respiratory polio, unable to breathe without respiratory equipment, or to use hands and arms and needing everything to be done for her, gave a very vivid account of this. Although able-bodied attendants sometimes had difficulty in getting her in and out of bed and strapping on the chest respirator, one of her most competent attendants was a woman with "moderately severe" cerebral palsy: "with great concentration and effort she could control her spasms enough to get me in and out of bed, feed and aspirate me, strap on my chest respirator and start the generator when the power failed. When Phyllis first began these duties, it would take her a long time to complete them. In time she perfected them and could complete my care and housework routine as quickly as many able-bodied attendants...Phyllis brought a stability and dependability to my life that made it possible for me to do many things besides worry about who was going to help me. In return she received acceptance as a contributor to society, new confidence in her own abilities, social contacts and a modest income. We each gained the other as a friend."(13) In the same chapter Donna McGwinn also discusses the suitability of many mentally retarded individuals for attendant positions, and states that in the United States there is growing acceptance of their ability to help the physically disabled as more and more people in both groups attempt employment and independent living.

So far we have discussed only a few of the ways in which handicapped people can participate in volunteering. Most of them involved the giving of personal help to other disadvantaged members of the community, and there is clearly great scope for the more systematic development of schemes such as these for handicapped adults who cannot find employment. Even while still at school many handicapped as well as non-handicapped pupils could benefit from and enjoy going out into the community to give practical help of a great variety of kinds. However, the scope for voluntary work goes far beyond the offering of personal practical and other help. Other types of voluntary work in which unemployed handicapped people might wish to become involved include a whole range of social and civic organisations, political parties, pressure groups, and voluntary societies catering for disadvantaged, although not necessarily handicapped people.

Before leaving the question of volunteering, the very complicated issue of payment for "voluntary" work must be raised. It could be argued that if, for example, a mentally handicapped trainee in an Adult Training Centre copes responsibly with his "voluntary work" in a geriatric hospital, is he not, by definition, "employable"? Should the Centre not be training him to be fully competitive for employment? Is he not being exploited, particularly if his voluntary work occupies a substantial part of the working week? Undoubtedly some physically and intellectually handicapped individuals have shown, through "voluntary" work, that they were in fact already employable, while for others voluntary work has provided a variety of "work experiences" which gives them new skills so that they become employable. If this is the case, and if employment is their choice, that is what society should try to offer them.

The issue is, however, usually less clear-cut. Most volunteers, whether able-bodied or disabled, provide "services" of a kind which the statutory sector provides either inadequately or not at all; usually, it is argued, because such services are not (in terms of the resources available) priorities, i.e. society cannot afford to provide them. In helping to meet such needs, disabled people are no more being "exploited" than are able-bodied people who have time to give, and wish to use it in this way (provided, that is, that safeguards of the kind already mentioned are followed). In one sense the contribution of severely handicapped people to the voluntary sector can (as long as it is not misused) thus be looked on as another indication of their integration into society.

ADULT EDUCATION

Another whole area with great and unexplored potential for people unable to find employment or working only part-time or for shorter hours than in the past is that of adult education. The term is used here to encompass all the ways in which people may, throughout their lives, develop their intellectual, creative, physical and other abilities. In recent years, the concept of "permanent" or "continuing" education has been developing quite rapidly in a number of countries. For example, the U.K. Russell Report on Adult Education (1973)(2) envisaged a "society in which the whole life-long learning needs of all citizens would be taken as the field with which the national educational system is concerned in its basic planning structures and expenditure". A major idea of this report was that there should be expansion in the field of adult education and that it should enable people to build on their basic schooling in a wide variety of ways and in a flexible programme of courses, part-time, day release, evening, and so on. This was considered of particular importance in view of the high rate of unemployment.

Several of the disabled people who commented on this monograph believed that adult education offers considerable potential for enhancing the quality of life of people unable to find employment, and with this we are in full agreement. What must be emphasised however is that those with responsibility or an interest in developing opportunities in adult education for severely handicapped people should try to do this within the context of an expansion of adult education in society as a whole. Otherwise, there is a danger that, just as special education has developed in many countries in segregated settings and groups, the same may happen where adult education for handicapped people is concerned.

This means that everything possible should be done to facilitate the integration of physically and mentally disabled young people in local classes and groups, i.e. into the ordinary "integrated" adult education sector. At present, in many countries this is not done. In the U.K. Russell Report, concern was expressed about "those people hitherto untouched by adult education. Many of them are handicapped or disadvantaged in various ways, discouraged from participating in existing provision by their own limitations and circumstances, by unsuitable premises, by a sense of their own inadequacy". In other words, a combination of practical problems (especially transport, access and lack of information about what was available) as well as, in some cases, ambivalent feelings about joining "ordinary" classes and groups of various kinds, have meant that adult education has been least available to those who, in terms of the time at their disposal, could most benefit from and enjoy it.

Higher education, which usually includes the obtaining of further formal qualifications, is only one small area within the adult education field, but is an area in which technological change has offered exciting possibilities for many severely physically disabled people. For example, for very severely disabled people who find it difficult to travel, or who live in rural areas, distance teaching through the mass media (in particular in the United Kingdom, the Open University which makes a great deal of use of the telephone link-ups) and through correspondence, has opened up opportunities which give a new sense of purpose to life. The development of micro-processors, which we referred to earlier will accelerate these opportunities. To quote from a recent Central Policy Review paper, "self-teaching packages that can be used with a modified television set...are likely to grow steadily in popularity /and/ could represent a significant step in the development of technology for adult education. Their attraction will depend partly on the increasing amount of time which the individual will have at his own disposal". Developments in micro-electronics should also provide the disabled with much cheaper and more portable aids which can be operated even by those with extremely limited control of movement. One of the problems of distance teaching is that it does not solve the problem of social isolation, and it must be linked to group work and tutorial sessions, perhaps held on a short-term residential basis.

For most of the population, including the majority of handicapped people, "higher" education will be only a very small part of adult education. Much current thinking about the function of "day" and "training" centres stresses the need for a greater further education component than has hitherto been the case.

This can include further work in the basic subjects; education in social skills; and training for independent living. Such opportunities may need to be offered to young people until well into their twenties, as well as to older people, especially those moving from institutional to community living, and should, of course, involve the mentally handicapped(3) as well as the physically handicapped.

However, "further" education as used in this rather limited sense (i.e. of basic education in literacy and numeracy, and of social education) is only one aspect of adult education. In the short term, especially for school leavers, it may be of very great importance indeed, but in the long term, we think that of far greater importance are the opportunities which need to be provided to those living without work for engaging in a whole range of recreational pursuits. As noted earlier, improvements in transport, access, modifications to buildings and equipment and so on must be made so that handicapped people can use community facilities rather than attend classes in segregated centres, whether day or residential. Among these "recreational" pursuits sport is very important: many unemployed handicapped people would like to engage in sports on a regular basis (particularly, if they are severely disabled, swimming or riding), but either have no opportunity to do so, or no knowledge of local opportunities. Many would also like greater opportunities to take part in the creative arts such as pottery, painting, woodwork or photography. Other activities which continuing education should include are a whole range of pursuits (e.g. cookery, gardening, woodwork, simple electrical repairs and many other "do-it-yourself" skills which would enable young people and adults to look after and improve or even simply to pass on to others ideas about improving their own homes. In some cases skills or interests might be developed which could enable young people to create their own work at home, even if only on a small scale at first. This is a point we will develop further when considering a life based on the home.

In thinking about the kind of opportunities which should be offered, it is essential and also informative to try and get rid of preconceived ideas about what adult education should offer (these are often based on minority i.e. middle class preferences) and look at the ways in which the majority of non-handicapped people in a particular culture actually choose to spend their leisure. Recent surveys in the United Kingdom(19), for example, show that this is firstly in "casual", informal human intercourse", and secondly, the mass media. These are followed by "creative and utilitarian activities centred on the home". In other words, "popular culture in Britain is a domestic culture centring on the house and garden linked to the world outside by the car and TV". This may not be equally true of other countries, but those planning adult education opportunities for the handicapped need to take popular culture more seriously, especially in view of the increasing trend for disabled and intellectually impaired people to live as independently as possible in the community.

One very important aspect of adult education - and again, surveys show this is true for non-handicapped as well as for disabled people - is that the main motivation behind attending classes is most often social. The boredom and loneliness of many handicapped young people make this function of adult education doubly important for them and strengthens the argument that where possible handicapped people should use community facilities, or, if this is not possible, that residential and non-residential institutions which have or are planning to develop adult education programmes, should consider opening some of their classes to the community.

A HOME-BASED LIFE AS AN ALTERNATIVE TO WORK

In an article entitled "A 20 Hour Week"(4) Anatole Beck pointed out that "the fact that there are now more available workers than available jobs means we must find a way of limiting the length of the working week, or most people will find themselves permanently jobless in early middle age." A solution was a "shortened, even drastically shortened work week." It would, he concludes, be "vastly preferable to work 20 hours a week for 40 years than 40 hours a week for 20 years. It could mean that men and women would have a place in the world of labour and yet still keep up their home life, which is one of the genuine and deep satisfactions which make life worth living."

In the case of severely disabled people the idea of "homemaking" as forming a satisfying alternative to employment is one which, until comparatively recently, would probably not have been taken seriously or considered feasible. Today, however, increasing numbers of severely physically and mentally handicapped people are beginning to live in their own homes in the community, rather than remaining with their families, and having as the only alternative to this placement a long-stay hospital, or other institution. For some of these people a life centred on running their own homes (with whatever help is necessary) and on living as independently as possible, may be more satisfying than going out every day to some sort of special centre for the handicapped or other people.

Homemaking as the central focus of life is particularly likely to be satisfying for disabled people who are married, or for those sharing a flat or house with one or two others. Susannah Miller(14), for example, in interviews with married couples one or both of whom were cerebral-palsied, has found that at least during the first years of marriage the new status which marriage confers and the fact that the young people now have, perhaps for the first time, all the interests which a home of one's own offers, often diminishes the need they feel to find employment. This new-found satisfaction may, however, be only temporary since a household which has no member in full-time employment cannot improve its financial situation. This meant, in her study, that disabled people sometimes felt that unless one or other could find work they could not afford to have children.

One solution is for individuals in this situation to seek out ways of supplementing their incomes by creating their own work which can be carried out at home. A very useful account of how various people - some disabled and some able-bodied - have achieved this is given in a recent booklet published by the Greater London Association for Initiatives in Disablement (GLAID)(12). The initiatives described by Micheline Mason range from those which bring in a little extra money to supplement other sources of income (e.g. benefits) to those which themselves provide very good incomes. The latter often began as hobbies and developed into flourishing businesses. Most of the activities described are crafts of various kinds requiring reasonable hand function (examples are making children's toys, wooden puzzles, doll's house furniture, clothes, machine-knitting, patchwork making, model-making, designing in stained glass and pewter, jewellery-making, restoring furniture, clock-repairing, offset lithoprinting and so on) but examples are also given of very severely disabled people carrying out business (e.g. accountancy) from home using electronic aids. The booklet has sections on how to acquire skills and training, on different ways of structuring work based on the home, on statutory legislation and on advisory organisations. While some of the practical information is, of course, only relevant to the United Kingdom, many of the ideas are of much wider relevance, and similar booklets could be produced in other countries.

At present the option of having one's own home is still, in most countries, open to only a small minority of severely handicapped people. Schemes such as ENCOR in Nebraska(9) or others run on similar lines are opening up this possibility to mentally handicapped people. In the case of physically and multiply handicapped people, purpose-built housing and physical care may both be needed. Sweden has pioneered the way with its Fokus scheme, now run by the State. The philosophy behind the scheme is that the only people who know how the disabled want to live are disabled people themselves, and that the State has the obligation to do all it can to meet these demands. The Fokus flats are purpose-built but scattered through normal housing blocks all over the country. Staff are available at any time the residents require help, with housewives paid to come in at the "peak" morning, evening and lunch-time hours. Shearer, in an article on housing for the handicapped[18] notes that over three-quarters of its tenants were in wheelchairs and a third needed turning and help every night in going to the toilet. The existence of such a scheme has changed the life of many of its tenants: "over a third of them are now either married or living together - before they came here the proportion was under 10 per cent. Only a quarter of the population is housebound: the rest either work or are completing their studies. Before they lived here, a third were in their family home, and the rest in nursing homes and other institutions." Other countries have now begun to follow this lead.

Apart from purpose-built housing, the other main need of severely handicapped people living in their own homes is for regular physical help. This has to be provided on a statutory basis, but there is also considerable scope for the giving and receiving of informal help. Relatives and neighbours are one important source of such help; Miller[14] for instance found that parents who were hostile to the idea of a disabled young person getting married frequently changed their attitudes once the marriage became a _fait accompli_, and became extremely helpful.

Self-help schemes also have an important part to play. A useful model is the scheme launched by the U.K. voluntary organisation, Age Concern. Although designed for retired people, many of its ideas could be developed either through the personal contacts of disabled individuals, or by users of centres for the disabled, for example day centres. The scheme, which is called Link Opportunity, enables retired people, in association with young members of the community to continue using their skills and knowledge for _mutual_ benefit. Although Link schemes are locally based, and operate differently in different parts of the country, they are run on the principle of the barter system, where no money changes hands. A dressmaker, for example, turns a collar and has her grass cut in return. The scheme works through the issue of token stamps. Anyone in the local scheme can earn stamps by performing some sort of useful service and then "spend" the stamps in getting a job done by someone who is on Link's central register. The sorts of skills exchanged have included baby-sitting, minor car repairing, care of pets, carpeting, chess, cooking, correspondence, electrical repairs, house decorating and repairs, knitting, laundry, music, needlework, plumbing, reading aloud, shopping, collecting library books and prescriptions, tax aid, transport, tuition of all kinds, typing and visiting.

The idea has spread from the United Kingdom to Canada, Australia and Belgium, and Age Concern has just produced an "Action Guide" designed to advise those interested and involved in the setting up of Link job exchanging schemes(1). Whether having token stamps is necessary or even desirable in any such scheme is a question that might be examined.

Severely handicapped people leading a life based on the home are in danger, as are many young housewives, elderly people and others, of suffering from boredom and loneliness, especially if one of the marriage partners, or the parents of a young person living in the family home, goes out to work. An advantage of the Link Scheme is that it can widen social contacts. It must be emphasised here that for severely handicapped people telephone contacts are also of very great importance, and it has been suggested that in the future, with developments in micro-electronics, it may be possible to establish contacts with neighbours and with other disabled people through local television networks. Certain facilities for study, or for creative and recreational activities could also be provided within the home, for example by domiciliary craft instructors or adult education tutors for those who do not wish to go out, or have great difficulty in doing so.

Even those who have chosen a life in which the home is the main interest need to get out regularly. The suggestions made earlier about voluntary work and adult education are of relevance here: a mix of activities of these kinds can help a home-based individual to build up a varied life with a definite structure to it.

There is also a need to develop more flexible forms of day provision than at present generally exists. Most day training centres or their equivalents offer an "all or none" service, i.e. users attend for a specified number of hours per week or not at all. Staffing, transport, programmes, meals, etc. are geared to this, and it is obviously much more difficult to be flexible. However, the Stone House Centre which we are about to describe shows that it is possible to run a centre which people can attend as and when they feel the need to.

A COMMUNITY WORK APPROACH - THE STONE HOUSE

We end this section on ideas for alternatives to work with a short account of an innovative approach to meeting the needs of disabled people within a local authority centre, which had integration as a central part of its policy. The authors of the report on this scheme(22), who jointly set up and managed this centre for its first five years, sum up its relevance in their statement: "We do not believe we found the whole answer to the problem of providing meaningful alternatives to work, but we think we started something which could go quite a long way towards doing so."

The Stone House was originally planned as a "day centre for the handicapped and elderly" in a small location of heavy industry (population 50,000) in the Midlands of England. The couple who eventually took the responsibility for running it (one a social worker, the other a teacher, and both with experience of community work) were able to develop innovative practices. Their philosophy was to concentrate attention on the needs of disabled people, while having an "open door" policy to others in the community, for example relatives and friends of the users, as well as the parents of handicapped children, and also other people with special needs, provided that they were under 60 years old on arrival, and "intellectually capable of organising their own lives" within the context of the centre. This was interpreted generously and users included a few people who were mentally ill or who had previously attended centres for the mentally handicapped. The "house style" was informal; the aim was that no one, on crossing the threshold, should feel anyone's "client" or "patient" or anything other than "a person who was able to manage his own affairs". Users were given as much independence as possible, within the limits of their disabilities and a minimum of organised help, in order to encourage self-help and to foster a community spirit.

At the end of five years there were about 100 people using the centre in the course of a week (some came daily, others much less frequently) of whom about 60 were disabled. Most users were under 45 years old and some were in their late teens and early twenties. There were two full-time staff (Manager and Deputy Manager), two part-time care assistants, two part-time drivers, as well as a part-time secretary, caretaker and two cleaners, while a craft instructor came for six hours each week.

The rationale for the centre was the belief that disabled people (particularly those who become disabled later in life) and parents with handicapped children often find it helpful to share the company and experience of others with similar problems. An important function of the centre was the continuing education of both users and staff on general developments concerned with the welfare of disabled people. Users were also given specific information about their own disabilities and the kind of help available to them. Attempts were also made to educate the local community (both children and adults, including professionals) about disability, so that the centre was a source of expertise.

While the focus was on disability, the "open door" policy was considered of equal importance. The majority of disabled people do not wish to spend most of their time in the company of others who are disabled; they want to meet people who share their individual interests and preoccupations. For this reason, provided that they came, as it were, on the terms of the disabled members, non-disabled people were able to join in the activities of the centre, while the disabled users were encouraged to make a fulfilling life for themselves outside the centre (and, through a very flexible transport system, were enabled to do so). The managers were more concerned if a user had no social life outside the centre than if he or she was only an occasional user of it.

The organisers rejected as "exploitation" (the word expresses their strong feelings) the possibility of sub-contract work, which is difficult to combine with other activities. They thought rather of "meaningful and pleasurable activity" but had no highly structured programme, aiming rather to "create a social ambience in which people felt confident enough to try a wide range of activities and to help each other achieve certain goals". Some of the activities had an element of what we described earlier as "volunteering"; users might do toy repairs for the toy library, make something for the playgroup, build a piece of equipment for the centre, help an aphasic user practise his speech or reading, or help prepare the midday snack. Other activities were more purely recreational, for instance, making something for one's own home. Regular activities, with which some of the disabled users helped but which benefited or involved other members of the local community included a telephone information service on disability, a toy library for handicapped children, a mixed play group and a youth club.

An important aspect of the Stone House experiment was the policy on transport. The main aim was to provide a service which could meet the individual requirements over which the users themselves had as much control as possible. To achieve this without increasing overall costs, planned allocation of resources was shifted from meals to transport (i.e. a midday snack was provided instead of a large meal). People were encouraged and enabled to come and go as they wished - in terms of when they were picked up in the morning, when they went home, and where they went, from the centre, during the day. Although this ideal was never completely realised, as there were many conflicting needs, considerable flexibility was achieved, and the centre's organisers were able "to transport any disabled person almost anywhere at any time of the day".

Normally, the transport available consisted of two 12-seater minibuses (with tail-lifts and anchor points for wheelchairs) and two part-time drivers who worked up to 30 hours a week. The buses were also made available at any time (including evenings or weekends) to any organisation with disabled members or to disabled individuals who wanted and needed them and could provide their own drivers.

The two drivers were key personnel, and were encouraged to take instructions directly from their passengers. As the number of users of the centre grew, pressure on the drivers built up. The scheme's organisers came to the conclusion that the problems which such a flexible system gives rise to would be lessened if the part-time jobs of the drivers were expanded to full-time, and the post of driver was combined with that of care-assistant. This would show the drivers how the driving aspect of the job fitted in with the general care for people's welfare which was the aim of the centre.

The scheme's organisers thought two main developments were most needed in the future. One was an expansion of adult education, through improved links with the local Adult Education Department and the creation of two new posts, those of craft-instructor and adult education tutor, who would divide their time between the Stone House and domiciliary visits. The other was the setting up of an assessment unit at the centre, to assess the everyday needs of an individual and his family and the problems faced by them within their own community, together with an appraisal of the resources available to them. Such an assessment would involve an examination of the full range of interests of the disabled person, including both work and leisure and the best way he or she could pursue these interests.

USING THE EXISTING FRAMEWORK OF PROVISION

Young handicapped individuals and their families may wish to explore some of the suggestions made hitherto and will probably also have ideas and experiences of their own to add about the ways in which a life without work can be enriched. A more far-reaching question, however, is how these kinds of suggestions might be put into practice without too much difficulty. A number of the guiding principles which might be followed are suggested below.

There should be much more client participation in the running of day and residential centres, hostels and homes for the disabled, and so on. All users and staff should have the opportunity of participating jointly in the running of the centre and in planning a programme of activities. Some centres may decide to do this through committees, while others, particularly small centres, may hold regular meetings (e.g. on a weekly basis) which <u>all</u> staff and users attend. At present there appears to be surprisingly little systematically organised client participation. In the Schlesinger study(17), for example, 80 per cent of those interviewed thought that the work centres they attended should have a planning committee (for discussing general principles, details of day-to-day management, suggestions for improvements, the welfare of clients and so on) but only 3 out of the 26 centres had one. It has to be recognised that the ability to contribute to or run a committee and to participate in planning a centre's activities may require both training and experience, and that it may be one of the roles of a centre to provide this.

All those involved in the setting up and running of centres for particular groups, for instance for physically handicapped or multiply-handicapped young people, or for the elderly, should be fully conscious of the fact that such centres can, by their very existence and even if set up with the best of intentions, have segregating effects, and that everything possible should be done to counteract this tendency. This will not be achieved unless the staff see one of their main functions as being to help clients to make use of ordinary facilities in the community and to enter as fully as possible into its life. This does not mean that all or even most programmes of training, social education, further education and creative and recreational activities within the centre should be discontinued. It does mean, however, that centres should have an outward-looking philosophy rather than attempt to provide within themselves all the facilities that their clients might wish.

This has clear implications for the initial and in-service training and status and hence the pay of the staff employed in such centres. The approach we are advocating will put considerable demands upon staff. It is much more difficult, although ultimately probably more rewarding, for staff to seek continually for ways of involving their users in the local community than it is simply to organise activities within a centre. The staff will often be faced by unsympathetic or stereotyped public attitudes about handicapped people and will only succeed if those trying to achieve innovations in existing practice are clear about their goals and have been given detailed guidance about how to achieve these.

Staff need also to be prepared for the fact that many of the clients of a centre will need encouragement and guidance if they are to become interested and involved in activities outside the centre. In the

Schlesinger study(17) although many clients were able to say how they would like to use their time "a large number had insufficient experience to appreciate the possibilities open to them or even to know what their own interests were, or what their handicaps would allow them to do, and needed guidance and help." It will thus be one of the main roles of the staff to help their clients to discover, to develop and to use their interests and skills, not only within the centre, but also in the community outside. If staff are to help them in this they will need a very detailed knowledge of the facilities available in that locality and an acknowledged part of their jobs should be to build up and maintain contacts with the community. One way of doing this is to involve volunteers from the community who share the individual clients' interests and can accompany them to classes in the community or support them, at least initially, in voluntary work.

Centres should play an enabling role in helping users to engage in a wide range of adult education activities of the kinds discussed earlier. While these should be provided mainly outside the centre, certain activities may be based within it but staffed at least in part by teachers and instructors from outside. Activities based within the centre may, in particular, include the training of users in self-help skills which will enable those who are not already doing so to live independently in the community, or, if living with their parents, to do more for themselves at home.

Individual members of a centre should have the freedom to choose the activities they wish to engage in and to make personal arrangements to take part in activities outside the centre. If this is to be achieved, and if substantial numbers of a centre's users are to be involved in community activities such as adult education or voluntary service on a larger scale than has been usual hitherto, the centre will need to have at its disposal a very flexible system of transport. In every survey of the disabled, transport comes up as an obstacle which prevents many disabled people from taking part in voluntary work, day and evening classes, work sharing schemes, and so on. Since it is so crucial, detailed accounts of how a flexible system can be organised, both for urban and rural areas, would be valuable.

While we have laid great emphasis on users going out into the community from centres, another way of counteracting the segregating effects of centres is to encourage people from the community to come in. Thus, although the major focus of a particular centre may be upon a specific group, such as young disabled adults, it may also be able to function as a community centre rather than simply as a centre for the handicapped, i.e. it should be open to other users from the community. Who these are will vary according to local needs, but the principle is that as many activities as possible should be integrated, since there are advantages in this both for the disabled and for the able-bodied. One danger which has been pointed out to us is that if services for other members of the community with special needs, for example the mentally ill, are inadequate, a centre with a fairly open policy may become overweighted by a particular "problem group" so that the purpose of opening it up to other community members, i.e. of making it as "normal" a place as possible, is defeated. The example of the community centre in Corby(3) suggests, however, that it is possible to achieve the right sort of mix, and also that a small town with a population of about 50,000 will have in it enough potential users to make a centre viable.

Finally, and we would like to place great emphasis on this point, centres should, wherever this is appropriate, and if it is the wish of the users, take much more active steps to prepare the clients for open and sheltered employment, as well as helping them to explore and use local and regional facilities for vocational training. Staff and clients should also systematically explore local opportunities for part-time paid employment, shared work and similar schemes.

IMPLICATIONS FOR SERVICE PROVISION

If, as we believe, increasing numbers of handicapped people are likely to spend large parts (if not all) of their lives without work, there are major implications for what is done at school and after school to prepare them for this possibility. At present few special schools or classes tackle this question in any but the most perfunctory way, and handicapped adolescents may leave school totally unprepared for the idea that they may never work and also without the resources which would enable them to cope with this reality or to take advantage of the alternatives. (A similar situation exists in the case of those soon to retire, and many organisations for the elderly now run pre-retirement preparation schemes or are pressing for these to be set up.)

One thing, therefore, that we feel schools should be doing is to prepare young people for the idea that they may not be able to find employment and to discuss with them, while they are still at school, possible alternatives. Such preparation has both practical and psychological aspects. On the practical side possible alternatives should not simply be discussed theoretically but visits should be made to centres in the community, film and video-tape used, disabled young adults who are living without work invited to the school or college to discuss their experience with the students, and so on. Everything possible should be done to interest students in aspects of the local community in which they might be able to become involved, even if they are unable to find work, and much more could be done by schools to identify and develop at an earlier age aptitudes and interests. Young people also need guidance while at school in how to structure their time. Even if there is some prospect of eventual employment, many handicapped young people pass their holidays, college vacation and periods in which they may be searching for a job, or be between jobs, in a state of isolation, boredom and depression, the question of how they might spend such periods having never been discussed with them or their parents by school staff, social workers or other professionals.

Preparation for life without work will also, in the case of many pupils, involve group discussions and individual counselling to help them express and discuss their feelings about the possibility of not being able to work, so that this does not come as a complete shock to them after they have left school. Parents will also need to be closely involved in such preparation. Clearly it is both unfair and unrealistic to expect young people and their parents to be able to "accept" or "come to terms" with the fact that they may be very unlikely to find work as long as society (and that will include schools, whether ordinary or special) is still imbued with the work ethic. Also, many handicapped young people who appear likely to be unemployable may develop new skills in their late teens or twenties which may make them employable, or changing attitudes in society and changing technology may open up to them new opportunities. However, the whole issue needs to be aired and discussed much more openly, both at school and afterwards, than has been the case in the past, and the staff of schools and colleges need training if they are to be able to do this effectively.

One example of a college for disabled post-16-year-olds which is trying to face up to the fact that many of its leavers will not be able to get employment is Beaumont College in Lancaster, England. This college, first opened in 1977 by the U.K. Spastics Society for slow learning multi-handicapped cerebral-palsied leavers, has given a great deal of thought to an innovative curriculum(6). The curriculum is concerned with three main areas: (i) continuity and development of basic skills of numeracy and language development; (ii) identification and development of vocational skills and aptitudes; and (iii) delineation and development of social skills and behaviour, especially in the areas of personal competencies and interpersonal relationships. The distinguishing feature of the curriculum is the emphasis given to the last of these. It recognises that non-handicapped people need "social education" in their interaction with the non-handicapped as much as or more than do the handicapped. However, given that social barriers do exist, handicapped school leavers need to be helped to learn how to deal with negative social attitudes which may effectively bar them both from work and from some of the alternatives (e.g. volunteering, ordinary adult education) discussed in this paper. Students are thus encouraged to develop strategies and social skills which will enable them to operate more successfully in situations where, because of their visible and severe handicaps, they are likely to be misunderstood, ignored or even ostracised. Preparation at Beaumont for a life which may be one without work also includes helping students to acquire an independent status within the family or institution; the identification and development of leisure and recreational aptitudes and interests; the development of the individual student's awareness of the contribution he or she can make to society; discussions of how local facilities and agencies can be used, and so on.

We have mentioned earlier the need which almost all of us have for routines and socially imposed expectations to help structure our lives and focus our activities. If one is to sustain an activity, to make an effort, to persist in the face of difficulties or when things get boring, one requires a goal at which to aim, towards which to strive. But it is a very rare person who defines his own goals and presses on toward their accomplishment irrespective of public opinion or the approval of others. Most of us are sustained by the support of family or friends, by the sanctions and rewards of teachers or employers, and by the examples set by peers or society in general. A problem which besets those who plan - or take - non-vocational leisure time or educational courses is how to provide the extrinsic motivation that will keep the students going when interest flags. By and large the more abstract or academic the activity the more remote are the ends for which it is pursued. Practical activities, properly taught, can bring immediate rewards: after one lesson in carpentry you can nail two pieces of wood together to make an aeroplane even though you cannot make a bookcase or a wooden stool.

In speaking about leisure activities, we have emphasised that they should be pursued voluntarily. This does not mean however that no persuasion should be brought to bear on those who enlist to take them; nor does it mean that those who are prepared to sit back and have others do for them things which they could well do for themselves should not have this pointed out to them. The doctrine that "if a men will not work neither shall he eat" is too harsh and too inhuman to be tolerable. But a necessary complement to the entirely justifiable demand of handicapped people that they be given their rights as adults to manage their own lives and be accorded proper respect and consideration is that they should fulfil the social obligations which such rights entail.

The suggestions made here about alternatives to work cannot be implemented without fundamental changes in the attitudes to and perceptions of society as regards its handicapped members and the role they could play. There is often a vicious circle here. Society (e.g. a local authority official, a potential employer, even a voluntary organisation) is afraid to give a handicapped person an opportunity to shoulder greater responsibility (whether this is in living independently, or in using a centre's kitchen unsupervised or in doing a part-time job or, for that matter, full-time employment) in case that individual cannot cope, while the handicapped individual cannot break out of his sterotyped role because of lack of opportunity or because he has come to accept society's valuation of him. A similar problem exists in the case of other groups. For example, society both at the local authority and the individual level tends to have stereotyped views about what activities elderly people prefer, and assigns them a much more passive role than is merited. It is thus often extremely difficult both for handicapped people and for forward-looking (and often badly paid) staff in the centres which provide for them to make even minor changes in the directions we have indicated.

Also, as we implied earlier, the very existence of separate centres for particular groups does, however innovative they are (and those which are innovative are comparatively few), tend to reinforce society's expectations and stereotypes. We have tried, in this report, to take account of the sorts of structures and institutions which exist, and to look at ways in which their role might be developed and their relationship with the wider community made much closer, but perhaps the whole concept of "centres" is wrong. Certainly, much more consumer-oriented research is needed, directed by or in close collaboration with disabled people, to find out exactly what sort of structured day provision is wanted and needed by those unable to find work as well as those who choose not to work. In the United States the movement towards self-determination on the part of the disabled has been much stronger than in many European countries: an example of this is the Center for Independent Living (CIL) founded in 1972 in Berkeley, California. This is an innovative and comprehensive programme created and directed by and for persons who are severely physically disabled or blind, which aims to increase, through a wide range of supportive services, the mobility, opportunities and independence of those whom it serves.

What cannot be denied is that if handicapped people are to lead satisfying and dignified lives without work they will, like other members of society who are not wage earners, be particularly dependent for their whole well-being on the quality of the services which society is willing to provide for them. Service provision has been discussed elsewhere but we would underline the particular importance, for those living without work, of attractive purpose-built housing, close to public amenities; of "housekeeping" services, where required; of the availability throughout life of general help and advice (e.g. from a social worker, a health visitor, a neighbour, or a disability group); of adequate medical and nursing services; of improved access to public buildings, especially education and recreational facilities; and of a carefully thought-out policy on transport for the disabled. The other provision whose pros and cons were discussed earlier but which the authors see as essential, is a disablement benefit which is substantial enough to enable a severely handicapped person to choose not to work without being penalised financially.

REFERENCES

1. "Action Guide", Age Concern, England 1979.

2. Adult Education - A Plan for Development - Report of a Committee of Enquiry into Adult Education, HMSO, London, 1973.

3. Barayay E. A Life Time of Learning - A Survey of Further Education Facilities for Mentally Handicapped Adolescents and Adults, Royal Society for Mentally Handicapped Children, London, 1976.

4. Beck A. "A 20 Hour Week", New Society, 22 August 1974.

5. Beresford P. and Tuckwell P. "The Scandal of Adult Training Centres", Community Care, 2 August 1978.

6. Brindley A. Personal Communication, 1979.

7. Day Services for Mentally Handicapped Adults, Pamphlet No. 5, National Development Group for the Mentally Handicapped, HMSO, London, 1977.

8. Dickson M.E.A. "A Personal View", Social Work Today, Volume 8, No. 12, 1976.

9. "ENCOR - A Way Ahead", Campaign for the Mentally Handicapped Paper No. 6 CMH, 96 Portland Place, London, 1978.

10. Freeth Avril, Personal Communication, 1979.

11. Kaim-Caudle P. "The Sunderland Mobile Day Centre", University of Durham, Department of Sociology and Social Administration, 1977.

12. Mason M. Creating Your Own Work, Greater London Association for Initiatives in Disablement, Flat 4, Ramsden Road, Balham, London, 1978.

13. McGwinn D. Housing and House Services for the Disabled: Guidelines and Experiences in Independent Living, Harper and Low, Maryland, USA, 1977.

14. Miller S. Personal Communication, 1978.

15. North Yorkshire County Social Services Department. Personal Communication, 1978.

16. Oswin M. Children Living in Long-Stay Hospitals, Spastics International, Heinemann, 1978.

17. Schlesinger S. Industry and Effort: A Survey of Day Work Centres in England, Wales and Northern Ireland, The Spastics Society, London, 1977.

18. Shearer A. "Housing to Fit the Handicapped" in Boswell D. and Wingrove J. The Handicapped Person in the Community, Tavistock Publications, Open University Press, 1974.

19. Smith M.A., Parker S. and Smith C.S. Leisure and Society in Britain, Allen Lane, 1973.

20. Special Educational Needs. Report of a Committee of Enquiry into the Education of Handicapped Children and Young People, HMSO, London, 1978.

21. Topliss E. Provision for the Disabled, Basil Blackwell, 1975.

22. Tuckey L. and Tuckey B. "An Ordinary Place. The Stone House - A Community work approach to disabled people", unpublished manuscript.

23. Volunteer Centre - A Case in Point No. 2 - A Case Study of the provision of neighbourhood care for the house-bound, The Volunteer Centre, Berkhamstead, England, 1977.

24. Wolfenden Committee Report. The Future of Voluntary Organisations, Croom Held, London, 1978.

AN OVERVIEW OF THE PROJECT NOW COMPLETED

The innovations and examples of good practice described in the foregoing chapters have of course been developed against a background of worsening employment prospects in almost all developed countries; in the majority, the numbers of unemployed school leavers have multiplied with unprecedented rapidity since 1979. It is widely believed too that when the present worldwide recession eases jobs will not be much more readily available; many unskilled tasks and redundant skills no longer need to be performed. Clearly all this has serious implications for the employment prospects of those who are handicapped. Indeed, during the course of the CERI project, it has become evident that in many countries even those undergoing special work preparation schemes have less certain prospects.

By consequence of this, the alternatives to work canvassed in Tizard and Anderson's report have a particular - and indeed urgent - relevance. Many young people, whether disabled or not, now in effect receive a government "social wage" in return for socially useful "work" - rather than proper jobs - in a number of countries. Equally, voluntary work, particularly amongst women and those forced to retire early, is becoming an acceptable substitute in terms of self-justification and social usefulness as well as personal satisfaction. Consequently it may not be long before the disabled undertake occupations supported by a social wage without thereby feeling that they are second-class citizens. Nevertheless, it must always be remembered that the disabled are usually more dependent upon work than the rest of the community - not only for self-esteem and a secure place in society but also for friendships, broadening horizons and even finding a marriage partner.

In any case, for the foreseeable future the norm for the able-bodied will be a paid job, albeit, perhaps, with shorter hours or interspersed with periods of unemployment. As long as that is the norm, it behoves those responsible for delivering services to the young handicapped to make preparation for, and securing, work in as normal an environment as possible a primary objective.

The experiences described in the foregoing schemes vary considerably, as is inevitable given social, economic and political differences between countries, the variety and severity of handicaps and other variables. Nevertheless, some conclusions can be drawn as to the most effective way to provide for handicapped adolescents.

The acquisition of the basic skills of literacy and numeracy together with personal development which encompasses relationships with others are necessary social skills for those with and without handicaps alike. Indeed the emphasis on communication may need to be particularly strong in early adolescence for young people with particular disabilities. Yet in no sense must the curriculum be narrow or restricted to the bounds of the classroom or school. Inevitably many adolescents with handicaps have a more restricted social life outside school than their contemporaries. Therefore it is especially important that in their final years at school they are given opportunities to go out into the community and develop confidence in coping with transport, traffic, shopping and so on. Similarly, in the developing countries life is more sophisticated and complex than ever so the school programme often now includes knowledge of a wide range of welfare and financial procedures such as banking, pensions benefits and social and community services. Perhaps less universal and less well developed is the introduction of adolescents who are handicapped to leisure and recreational activities they can pursue beyond school. School in many countries provides a bridge so that young people can continue their interest in a youth or sports organisation once they leave it. There is frequently a similar need to extend cultural interests in the immediate post-school years. This is just one example of compartmentalised service delivery for the young who are disabled. So often schools, youth organisations and other organisations are making provision in relative isolation from each other, even where their facilities are physically adjacent.

The third key aspect within the curricula during the final two years at school (which, of course, vary between countries from the 14-16 to 18-19-year-olds) is clearly a familiarisation with the world of work. In recent years, specific vocational preparation at school has been less well regarded and seen as restricting possibilities rather than enhancing them, except perhaps for the severely handicapped. More common is a programme designed to introduce the youngster to the disciplines of the work place, to ensure he knows what will be demanded of him and to give him general facilities - in, for example, motor skills, office practice or whatever. The importance of careers education aimed at informing youngsters of available opportunities in a realistic way and of individual careers counselling now appears to be universally acknowledged.

Central to curriculum planning in the last year of school and appropriate counselling and guidance is a multi-disciplinary reassessment around the time transition is being planned. At this stage those concerned with vocational preparation and with seeking and securing employment can comment on the appropriateness of the course for the individual and begin to plan their contribution to transition. This demands staff inside and outside schools with knowledge of employment and community services and ability to assist the social transition from school to adult life. Careers teachers or counsellors will also need to understand the implications of different disabilities for adult and working life. The degree of assessment, counselling guidance and course planning which is possible in separate special schools is more difficult to reproduce in all mainstream schools where individuals with disabilities may be placed and some grouping within selected high schools often occurs to overcome this. However, the availability of adequate numbers of careers teachers or counsellors is vital, since all too often lack of appropriately skilled staff means that counselling may be confined to the final year before leaving school or to the most urgent cases, and subsequent follow-up may be sketchy.

Even in those countries with the most extensive provision at the post-school stage and those with the highest proportion in education and training to 18 or 19 years of age, there is considerable variation in the availability and quality of options for the school leaver. Very rarely are the needs of the handicapped adolescent assessed in terms of his adult life during the key years between 14 and 19 or 20. Still less frequently are there reassessments by multi-disciplinary teams making written proposals for meeting his needs later - employment, residence, social support, recreational, medical, etc. Yet there is a widespread acceptance that this process is fundamental to adequate service delivery; apart from everything else it would highlight as never before the grave deficiencies of support services for the adolescent and adult disabled in most parts of most countries.

Previous chapters have demonstrated that it is after the handicapped have left school that the most fundamental changes have occurred in recent years. In many countries - the United Kingdom is an outstanding example - provision for the handicapped school leaver is traditionally the most deficient aspect of all educational provision. But under the stimulus of increasing unemployment, and pressure from interest groups, many more special work preparation courses have been established. The examples described earlier in France, Norway, Sweden, Italy and the United Kingdom obviously differ in scope, length and to some extent intention but the basic motivation is common, to enhance the young person's employability and to smooth his path into a job.

It is possible to discern some pre-requisites for success. Firstly, the scheme must be designed with a full knowledge of what the youngsters have received at school. Sometimes post-school curricula are simply a repeat of the basic educational and life and social skill training which the student may have undertaken during his last two years at school.

Secondly, progression is most effective, if gradual, from college classroom or workshop to a protected working environment, perhaps within the environs of an educational establishment, and thence into open employment. The pace needs to be related to the individual, and rigidity in course planning must thus be avoided.

Tutors must prepare potential employers to accept handicapped young people who may need a modified working environment and may not be able to achieve normal levels of productivity, at least immediately. Equally, future workmates will be more ready to accept the disabled on equal terms if they have had contact with those responsible for the preparation courses.

For some who are severely handicapped open employment may not, currently, be an option in all countries. Yet everywhere the pressure on sheltered employment openings becomes more acute. Not only are more profoundly handicapped surviving to adulthood, but the inability of those with more moderate handicaps to secure employment increases the bids. Often, sheltered workshops are criticised because of the restricted and repetitive nature of the work and because they do little or nothing to 'normalise' the living of the disabled. Yet this should not be seen as an argument not to extend the number of places or, indeed, to reduce them, but rather to ensure that for the future sheltered workshops are more attractive, sociable and have the facility to provide a general educational and recreational function. There is a need for more centres or industrial enclaves providing extended employment as nearly as possible on an economic basis but without turning their workforce into automatons.

There is some ambivalence as to whether positive discriminatory policies in favour of employing the disabled are helpful. We have seen that the United States government insist, as a condition of letting contracts, that firms must employ a proportion of disabled people and the United Kingdom has its quota system. Yet, understandably, registration is distasteful to many disabled workers who prefer to be regarded as members of the workforce on their merits. On the other hand, published policies by public sector employers can be helpful not only directly to disabled applicants but also in reassuring co-workers and managers. Various contributions seem to suggest that a high proportion of employment opportunities are in the public sector rather than private enterprises in many countries.

The International Year of the Disabled underlined that problems of physical access are universal. New designs for buildings and street networks sometimes, but still not always, take account of this, but the fundamental problem is in trying to deal with the 'backlog' of centuries of building on the assumption that all potential users are sound in wind, limb, mind, sight and hearing. Much greater public and private investment is necessary to enhance access to public buildings and employment.

Throughout the CERI project - and this is reflected in earlier chapters - there is a commitment to the importance of teamwork - among doctors, psychologists, special teachers, social workers, therapists of all kinds. Yet intra-professional jealousies are seldom difficult to discover, often rooted in a conscientious belief that a particular approach is 'right' and in the best interests of those who are handicapped. Most of the examples described earlier are based upon fruitful co-operation and planning by multi-disciplinary groups determined to see, and cater for, the needs of the whole young person. Nevertheless, perhaps the greatest step forward, and one which need not cost money, is to improve communications. In 1980 an experienced United Kingdom commentator on provision for the handicapped adolescent was impelled to write " there is an astonishing ignorance at all levels of what other people are doing". It is evident that in this respect the United Kingdom is not unique.

Examples of good practice abound throughout the world, yet one lesson of the project to date is that so often what has been developed remains unknown even to those operating in a similar field in the same country. Indeed, those teaching 15-year-olds may know little of the workplace to which the handicapped youngster graduates - and vice versa. Inevitably, only a small proportion of those responsible for managing or providing services for the handicapped can be involved in a project of this kind; and it is likely that many outstanding examples have simply been missed in this survey. The overriding question, therefore, must be, how can the delivery of services be influenced for the better by the dissemination of experience elsewhere? In every country there is some good provision of some kind, a sheltered workshop, a multi-disciplinary team, a committed and determined employer, and usually this excellence depends upon one person or a group of people. Equally, most if not all countries have vast tracts of under-provision or non-existent provision, particularly in relation to the immediate compulsory post-school years. The common standard cannot be made to approximate to that of the outstanding in any country in a short span. But groups within countries and across boundaries must continue to learn from each other and press for the resources and investment - and often the appropriate legislative framework - to ensure that all handicapped young people are able to live the fullest achievable lives in the 'least restrictive environment'.

OECD SALES AGENTS
DÉPOSITAIRES DES PUBLICATIONS DE L'OCDE

ARGENTINA – ARGENTINE
Carlos Hirsch S.R.L., Florida 165, 4° Piso (Galería Guemes)
1333 BUENOS AIRES, Tel. 33.1787.2391 y 30.7122
AUSTRALIA – AUSTRALIE
Australia and New Zealand Book Company Pty, Ltd.,
10 Aquatic Drive, Frenchs Forest, N.S.W. 2086
P.O. Box 459, BROOKVALE, N.S.W. 2100
AUSTRIA – AUTRICHE
OECD Publications and Information Center
4 Simrockstrasse 5300 BONN. Tel. (0228) 21.60.45
Local Agent/Agent local :
Gerold and Co., Graben 31, WIEN 1. Tel. 52.22.35
BELGIUM – BELGIQUE
CCLS – LCLS
19, rue Plantin, 1070 BRUXELLES. Tel. 02.521.04.73
BRAZIL – BRÉSIL
Mestre Jou S.A., Rua Guaipa 518,
Caixa Postal 24090, 05089 SAO PAULO 10. Tel. 261.1920
Rua Senador Dantas 19 s/205-6, RIO DE JANEIRO GB.
Tel. 232.07.32
CANADA
Renouf Publishing Company Limited,
2182 St. Catherine Street West,
MONTRÉAL, Que. H3H 1M7. Tel. (514)937.3519
OTTAWA, Ont. K1P 5A6, 61 Sparks Street
DENMARK – DANEMARK
Munksgaard Export and Subscription Service
35, Nørre Søgade
DK 1370 KØBENHAVN K. Tel. +45.1.12.85.70
FINLAND – FINLANDE
Akateeminen Kirjakauppa
Keskuskatu 1, 00100 HELSINKI 10. Tel. 65.11.22
FRANCE
Bureau des Publications de l'OCDE,
2 rue André-Pascal, 75775 PARIS CEDEX 16. Tel. (1) 524.81.67
Principal correspondant :
13602 AIX-EN-PROVENCE : Librairie de l'Université.
Tel. 26.18.08
GERMANY – ALLEMAGNE
OECD Publications and Information Center
4 Simrockstrasse 5300 BONN Tel. (0228) 21.60.45
GREECE – GRÈCE
Librairie Kauffmann, 28 rue du Stade,
ATHÈNES 132. Tel. 322.21.60
HONG-KONG
Government Information Services,
Publications/Sales Section, Baskerville House,
2/F., 22 Ice House Street
ICELAND – ISLANDE
Snaebjörn Jónsson and Co., h.f.,
Hafnarstraeti 4 and 9, P.O.B. 1131, REYKJAVIK.
Tel. 13133/14281/11936
INDIA – INDE
Oxford Book and Stationery Co. :
NEW DELHI-1, Scindia House. Tel. 45896
CALCUTTA 700016, 17 Park Street. Tel. 240832
INDONESIA – INDONÉSIE
PDIN-LIPI, P.O. Box 3065/JKT., JAKARTA, Tel. 583467
IRELAND – IRLANDE
TDC Publishers – Library Suppliers
12 North Frederick Street, DUBLIN 1 Tel. 744835-749677
ITALY – ITALIE
Libreria Commissionaria Sansoni :
Via Lamarmora 45, 50121 FIRENZE. Tel. 579751/584468
Via Bartolini 29, 20155 MILANO. Tel. 365083
Sub-depositari :
Ugo Tassi
Via A. Farnese 28, 00192 ROMA. Tel. 310590
Editrice e Libreria Herder,
Piazza Montecitorio 120, 00186 ROMA. Tel. 6794628
Costantino Ercolano, Via Generale Orsini 46, 80132 NAPOLI. Tel. 405210
Libreria Hoepli, Via Hoepli 5, 20121 MILANO. Tel. 865446
Libreria Scientifica, Dott. Lucio de Biasio "Aeiou"
Via Meravigli 16, 20123 MILANO Tel. 807679
Libreria Zanichelli
Piazza Galvani 1/A, 40124 Bologna Tel. 237389
Libreria Lattes, Via Garibaldi 3, 10122 TORINO. Tel. 519274
La diffusione delle edizioni OCSE è inoltre assicurata dalle migliori librerie nelle città più importanti.
JAPAN – JAPON
OECD Publications and Information Center,
Landic Akasaka Bldg., 2-3-4 Akasaka,
Minato-ku, TOKYO 107 Tel. 586.2016
KOREA – CORÉE
Pan Korea Book Corporation,
P.O. Box n° 101 Kwangwhamun, SÉOUL. Tel. 72.7369

LEBANON – LIBAN
Documenta Scientifica/Redico,
Edison Building, Bliss Street, P.O. Box 5641, BEIRUT.
Tel. 354429 – 344425
MALAYSIA – MALAISIE
and/et SINGAPORE - SINGAPOUR
University of Malaya Co-operative Bookshop Ltd.
P.O. Box 1127, Jalan Pantai Baru
KUALA LUMPUR. Tel. 51425, 54058, 54361
THE NETHERLANDS – PAYS-BAS
Staatsuitgeverij
Verzendboekhandel Chr. Plantijnstraat 1
Postbus 20014
2500 EA S-GRAVENHAGE. Tel. nr. 070.789911
Voor bestellingen: Tel. 070.789208
NEW ZEALAND – NOUVELLE-ZÉLANDE
Publications Section,
Government Printing Office Bookshops:
AUCKLAND: Retail Bookshop: 25 Rutland Street,
Mail Orders: 85 Beach Road, Private Bag C.P.O.
HAMILTON: Retail Ward Street,
Mail Orders, P.O. Box 857
WELLINGTON: Retail: Mulgrave Street (Head Office),
Cubacade World Trade Centre
Mail Orders: Private Bag
CHRISTCHURCH: Retail: 159 Hereford Street,
Mail Orders: Private Bag
DUNEDIN: Retail: Princes Street
Mail Order: P.O. Box 1104
NORWAY – NORVÈGE
J.G. TANUM A/S Karl Johansgate 43
P.O. Box 1177 Sentrum OSLO 1. Tel. (02) 80.12.60
PAKISTAN
Mirza Book Agency, 65 Shahrah Quaid-E-Azam, LAHORE 3.
Tel. 66839
PHILIPPINES
National Book Store, Inc.
Library Services Division, P.O. Box 1934, MANILA.
Tel. Nos. 49.43.06 to 09, 40.53.45, 49.45.12
PORTUGAL
Livraria Portugal, Rua do Carmo 70-74,
1117 LISBOA CODEX. Tel. 360582/3
SPAIN – ESPAGNE
Mundi-Prensa Libros, S.A.
Castelló 37, Apartado 1223, MADRID-1. Tel. 275.46.55
Libreria Bosch, Ronda Universidad 11, BARCELONA 7.
Tel. 317.53.08, 317.53.58
SWEDEN – SUÈDE
AB CE Fritzes Kungl Hovbokhandel,
Box 16 356, S 103 27 STH, Regeringsgatan 12,
DS STOCKHOLM. Tel. 08/23.89.00
SWITZERLAND – SUISSE
OECD Publications and Information Center
4 Simrockstrasse 5300 BONN. Tel. (0228) 21.60.45
Local Agents/Agents locaux
Librairie Payot, 6 rue Grenus, 1211 GENÈVE 11. Tel. 022.31.89.50
TAIWAN – FORMOSE
Good Faith Worldwide Int'l Co., Ltd.
9th floor, No. 118, Sec. 2
Chung Hsiao E. Road
TAIPEI. Tel. 391.7396/391.7397
THAILAND – THAILANDE
Suksit Siam Co., Ltd., 1715 Rama IV Rd,
Samyan, BANGKOK 5. Tel. 2511630
TURKEY – TURQUIE
Kültur Yayinlari Is-Türk Ltd. Sti.
Atatürk Bulvari No : 77/B
KIZILAY/ANKARA. Tel. 17 02 66
Dolmabahce Cad. No : 29
BESIKTAS/ISTANBUL. Tel. 60 71 88
UNITED KINGDOM – ROYAUME-UNI
H.M. Stationery Office, P.O.B. 569,
LONDON SE1 9NH. Tel. 01.928.6977, Ext. 410 or
49 High Holborn, LONDON WC1V 6 HB (personal callers)
Branches at: EDINBURGH, BIRMINGHAM, BRISTOL,
MANCHESTER, BELFAST.
UNITED STATES OF AMERICA – ÉTATS-UNIS
OECD Publications and Information Center, Suite 1207,
1750 Pennsylvania Ave., N.W. WASHINGTON, D.C.20006 – 4582
Tel. (202) 724.1857
VENEZUELA
Libreria del Este, Avda. F. Miranda 52, Edificio Galipan,
CARACAS 106. Tel. 32.23.01/33.26.04/31.58.38
YUGOSLAVIA – YOUGOSLAVIE
Jugoslovenska Knjiga, Terazije 27, P.O.B. 36, BEOGRAD.
Tel. 621.992

Les commandes provenant de pays où l'OCDE n'a pas encore désigné de dépositaire peuvent être adressées à :
OCDE, Bureau des Publications, 2, rue André-Pascal, 75775 PARIS CEDEX 16.
Orders and inquiries from countries where sales agents have not yet been appointed may be sent to:
OECD, Publications Office, 2 rue André-Pascal, 75775 PARIS CEDEX 16.

66145-2-1983

OECD PUBLICATIONS, 2, rue André-Pascal, 75775 PARIS CEDEX 16 - No. 42501 1983
PRINTED IN FRANCE
(96 83 01 1) ISBN 92-64-12438-1